HE GROWTH OF THE
LD TESTAMENT

H. Rowley

PER TORCHBOOKS ❧ The Cloister Library / TB 107 / $1.25

The Growth of the

OLD TESTAMENT

The Growth of the
OLD TESTAMENT

H. H. Rowley

Harper Torchbooks
The Cloister Library
HARPER & ROW, PUBLISHERS, NEW YORK AND EVANSTON

TO

PROFESSOR S. A. COOK

in token of gratitude
for countless gracious acts
of help and encouragement
and in recognition of all I owe
to the stimulus of his works
this little book is inscribed

THE GROWTH OF THE OLD TESTAMENT
Printed in the United States of America

This book was originally published in the Religion series of the Hutchinson University Library, edited by The Rev. Professor E. O. James, in 1950, and reprinted in 1953, 1956, 1958, 1960, and 1961. It is here reprinted by arrangement with Hutchinson & Co., Ltd. London.

First HARPER TORCHBOOK edition published 1963 by
Harper & Row, Publishers, Incorporated, New York and Evanston

CONTENTS

BOOK FIVE
THE CANON

PREFACE

At no time was it harder to write a book on this subject than the present, and every reader will want to criticize this one. Those who accept what were once referred to as 'the assured results of criticism' will complain that so much attention has been paid to other views; those who dissent from those views will complain that they have been again presented. It is my hope that both will feel that I have tried to give the reader, within the compass of a small volume, a fair picture of the state of present-day opinion. Not every view could be mentioned, of course, and I have tried to avoid presenting the reader with a maze of views through which he would have difficulty in making his way.

My own dissatisfaction is born of the many things that have had to be left out. Little space could be found for a discussion of the forms of Old Testament literature, and the principles and instruments of textual criticism have had to be left without mention. The chapter on the Canon is shorter than I could have wished, and the Apocrypha and Pseudepigrapha are so closely related to the Old Testament that I should have liked to give them some space. To do any of these things would have been possible only by sacrificing something else which seemed to me even more necessary.

It is a profound grief to me that Professor S. A. Cook died while this book was in the press. He had consented to allow me to dedicate it to him, and had seen the terms of the dedication, which I have left unchanged. I held him in deep affection, and owed him a debt of gratitude for innumerable kindnesses of which I am constantly sensible.

To Professor A. R. Johnson I am grateful for the service

of his eagle eye on the proofs, though with characteristic caution he disclaims responsibility for the use I have made of his help. To my daughter, Margaret, I am indebted for help in the preparation of the indexes.

H. H. ROWLEY.

Manchester University.

CHAPTER I

INTRODUCTION

THE Old Testament is a collection of sacred books gathered together by the Jews and adopted by the Christian Church as a part of its corpus of Scripture from its foundation. Certain other writings, not recognized by the Jews as canonical, were incorporated in Christian manuscripts of the Old Testament, and have been recognized as canonical in varying degree by some Christians. These latter will be referred to briefly in a later chapter, but the primary interest of the present volume will be limited to those books recognized by the Jews and universally recognized by the Christian Church as canonical. How they came to be regarded as canonical will be considered below. We shall first consider how they came into existence and assumed their present form.

This is by no means a simple study. Traditions of authorship became attached to some of the books in ancient times, and for long these traditions were accepted without question. That they involved many difficulties was recognized, but the task of scholarship was commonly regarded as the defence of the traditions, and great ingenuity was devoted to the explaining away of the difficulties. In modern times the books have been studied in complete independence of the traditions in an effort to determine their approximate date of composition, and conclusions diverging far from the traditions have been reached.

These conclusions were not reached speedily and universally. It was only gradually and after a long history of outmoded views that what is often called the "critical orthodoxy" that prevailed at the beginning of the present century became widely accepted. There were, indeed, always some who rejected the method of modern scholars in general, and who preferred to follow the older method of justifying the ancient traditions. In

recent years, however, there have been many challenges to
"critical orthodoxy" by scholars who accept the method
whereby it was established, and it is probable that the last
quarter of a century has seen a wider variety of views on many
Old Testament questions than any comparable period that has
preceded it. In few cases has any single challenge won a wide
following, so that "critical orthodoxy" can at most points claim
a greater following than any one of the alternative views that
have been reached by its method.

In a brief work such as the present, which aims to represent
present-day Old Testament scholarship, it is therefore necessary
still to present "critical orthodoxy" to the reader. At the same
time it is essential to give some account of the challenges, though
necessarily brief, since by their very number and variety they
indicate that modern theories are not without their difficulties.
To treat modern theories as the older traditions were so long
treated, as dogmas to be defended at all costs, whose difficulties
are to be resolved by special pleading in so far as they are openly
recognized at all, is to deny the modern method whereby they
were reached. It is wiser to recognize that, like all scientific
theories, they only hold the field until more satisfactory theories
are forthcoming, and that from the ferment of recent challenge
something more satisfactory may yet emerge, though in few
cases does it seem yet to have done so.

In recent years there have also been opened up new lines of
approach to the Old Testament, and some account of these
must be given, although again limits of space will impose
brevity of treatment. The aim of the writer throughout is not
to present his own views, but to acquaint the reader with the
present position of Old Testament scholarship on the time and
manner of compilation of the books of the Old Testament, yet
not in so bewildering a way that it will leave him with no clear
ideas. His emphasis will therefore be on the consensus of
opinion among sober scholars, though he will not present it as
the assured and unchallengeable view of modern scholarship
as a whole.

The order in which the books will be dealt with will be that
in which they stand in the Hebrew Bible. The English Bible
follows the order of some of the Greek manuscripts of the Old

Testament, though it differs from those manuscripts in separating into the Apocrypha those books not found in the Hebrew Canon, which are distributed amongst the others in the manuscripts. That the Hebrew Canon is the original canon of the Old Testament is generally agreed, though there have not been wanting some who have denied this. There are, however, no reasonable grounds for denying it, and it seems the most satisfactory basis for our study. That it does not represent the order in which the books were written will appear as we proceed, but the difficulties of attempting to deal with the books in the order in which they were written will equally appear.

The Hebrew Canon is divided into three parts, viz. the Law, the Prophets, and the Writings. The Law consists of the Pentateuch, traditionally regarded as the five books of Moses. The prophets are divided into the Former Prophets and the Latter Prophets. The Former Prophets consist of some of the books which we regard as the Historical books, viz. Joshua, Judges, the books of Samuel and Kings. The Latter Prophets consist of four prophetic collections, viz. Isaiah, Jeremiah, Ezekiel and the Twelve Minor Prophets. It will be observed that some of the books we regard as historical do not stand in this collection, and the book of Daniel, which we regard as a prophetic book, is not found with the other prophetic books. These all stand in the third division of the Canon, the Writings. This is a miscellaneous collection, consisting of Psalms, Proverbs, Job—known as the three poetical books, though there is much poetry in the Old Testament outside these books— the Song of Songs, Ruth, Lamentations, Ecclesiastes, Esther— known as the Five Rolls—Daniel, Ezra, Nehemiah and the books of Chronicles.

All of these books are written in Hebrew, save that a single verse of the book of Jeremiah and some chapters in Daniel and Ezra stand in Aramaic. The verse in Jeremiah (x. 11) is probably a gloss and not original to the book. The chapters in Ezra (iv. 8 to vi. 18, and vii. 12–26) are either extracts from an older source, or embody such extracts. The chapters in Daniel (ii. 4b to vii. 28) provide a problem for which no agreed solution has been found.

The text of the Old Testament has had a long history since

the books left the hands of the writers or editors who gave them their present form. For many centuries they were copied by hand, and despite the unusual care which they received involuntary errors inevitably crept in. Moreover, until long after the beginning of the Christian era the text contained no vowels, and many passages were capable of more than one interpretation. It cannot be taken for granted that when the vowels were added and a particular interpretation was therefore given to the text, this was the one originally intended by the writer. Into this question, and the means at our disposal for attempting a restoration of the text, we shall not go in the present work. Its importance to the student of the Old Testament is manifest, since all sound interpretation must start from the text intended by the writer, so far as it can be recovered. But the history of the text is somewhat aside from the subject now before us, which is concerned with the date and purpose and provenance of the books as they left the hands of their authors or of the compilers who gave them their present form.

It will be observed that it is not proposed to establish the authorship of the books of the Old Testament. This is not because questions of authorship lie outside our purpose, but because *we do not know the author of a single book of the Old Testament in the form in which it now stands*. Traditions of authorship will be examined, but in no case do they lead us to any assured identification of an author. In not a few cases we can be confident that we know the author of material found in books of the Old Testament, but in every case that material has been taken by another writer and issued in the form it now has. These writers, great creative artists, producing masterpieces of rich variety that are worthy to live as literature, were not concerned with their own undying fame. They were not artists for the sake of art, but men who were filled with a religious purpose, and who were consumed with that purpose. Whether their names lived or died was of no moment. But supremely important was it that they should guide men's feet in the way of God's will, and enrich them with understanding of His purpose.

BOOK I

THE LAW

CHAPTER II

THE PENTATEUCH

THE first five books of the Bible, traditionally ascribed to Moses, provide a brief sketch of human origins and an account of the history of the Israelite people to the death of Moses. Into this framework of history is fitted all that has come down to us of the ancient social and religious law of Israel, including the provisions for the ordering of the sacrificial cultus. The whole was compiled in a single work, whose division into five separate books was probably made later. By the Jews it is accorded a special sanctity, greater than that of the rest of the Old Testament, and it is the only part of the Old Testament which is recognized as canonical by the Samaritans. The individual books are known in Hebrew by their opening words, and in English by the names they bear in the Greek version.

The book of Genesis rapidly surveys the pre-Mosaic period, continually narrowing its interest so as to bring the story to the family of Jacob, leaving the accounts of the related and collateral peoples incomplete. Many of its stories reveal a moral sublimity that makes them of undying worth to men, and its accounts of the beginnings of the human race are shot through with profound and penetrating spiritual teaching. For it was written as a religious, rather than as a merely historical, work.

The book of Exodus begins with the birth of Moses, and tells how he led the Israelites out of Egypt to the sacred mountain, and instituted the sacred covenant there. It contains a corpus of ancient law, known as the Book of the Covenant, and gives a long account of the preparation of the Ark and the Tabernacle, with all the sacred furniture.

The book of Leviticus is mainly concerned with the regulations that governed the religious practice of Israel. It contains a section known as the Holiness Code, because of its

15

repeated summons to a holiness that consists in ritual purity
and moral worth.

The book of Numbers resumes the historical survey where
Exodus broke off, and carries the story through the period of
the Wandering to the conquest of Transjordan, but with
legislative material incorporated at various places, and the
Balaam Oracles included.

The book of Deuteronomy opens with a historical retrospect
attributed to Moses at the end of the period of the Wanderings,
followed by a Code of Laws which in part repeats and in part
modifies some of the legislative part of the earlier books. It ends
with the account of the death of Moses.

Whoever compiled the Pentateuch clearly believed that the
period of Moses was of supreme importance to Israel, as being
the period that saw the creation of the nation, and the foundation
of its religion and its institutions. It is believed by many
scholars that the sources used in the compilation of the Pentateuch were used also in the compilation of the book of Joshua,
and even of the succeeding historical books. But there is
no reason to suppose that the Pentateuch and Joshua ever
formed a single whole—a Hexateuch—and still less to suppose
that the Pentateuch and the later historical books ever formed
a single historical corpus.

(a) Sources and Compilation

The tradition that Moses was the writer of the Pentateuch
has been largely abandoned by modern scholars, and what is
frequently referred to as the Graf-Wellhausen hypothesis is
accepted in its place. Its acceptance does not involve the acceptance of all the ideas of those who first propounded it,
whether on the subject of the religious development of Israel or
on the principles of religious development in general. It is not
surprising that the evolutionary presuppositions of the nineteenth century should have influenced the form of its presenta-
tion in that age, but lying behind the work of Wellhausen was
the work of other writers who did not share those presuppositions, and who laid the real foundation for the modern theory.

The grounds on which the tradition of Mosaic authorship

is rejected are varied, and their weight is cumulative. They are here briefly summarized.

(1) On the theory of the Mosaic authorship, the Pentateuch contains a number of anachronisms. Some of these were anciently observed, and various suggestions have been made to account for them. The death of Moses is recorded in Deut. xxxiv. In Gen. xxxvi there stands a list of Edomite kings, and verse 31 states that these all reigned before Israel had a king— i.e., before the time of Saul. In Gen. xiv. 14, we read that Abram pursued the captors of Lot as far as Dan, yet according to Judges xviii. 29 this place was not known by that name until long after the time of Moses. The statement that the Canaanite was then in the land (Gen. xii. 6, xiii. 7) implies a time after the Israelite conquest of Canaan, and therefore after the time of Moses. There are several references to the Philistines in the Pentateuch (Gen. xxi. 34, xxvi. 14, 15, 18, Exod. xiii. 17), yet it is impossible to place Moses so late as the Philistine settlement in Palestine at the beginning of the twelfth century B.C. None of these anachronisms would occasion serious difficulty by themselves. For it might be supposed that later scribes had added explanatory glosses, or had modernized names.

(2) There are many duplications or triplications of incidents with curiously common features. Beersheba is so named to commemorate a covenant between Abraham and Abimelech according to Gen. xxi. 31, whereas according to Gen. xxvi. 31 the name found its origin in an incident that concerned Isaac and Abimelech. According to Gen. xxviii. 19, Jacob changed the name of Luz to Bethel when he was on his journey to Paddan-aram, while according to Gen. xxxv. 14 f. he set up the stone and gave the name to this place on his return many years later. His own name was changed to Israel by the divine wrestler at Peniel, according to Gen. xxxii. 28, while it was at Bethel according to Gen. xxxv. 10. Abram pretends that his wife is his sister and so deceives Pharaoh in Gen. xii. 10 ff., and in Gen. xx. 1 ff. he repeats this to impose on Abimelech, while according to Gen. xxvi. 6 ff. Abimelech is similarly deceived by Isaac. Hagar twice leaves her mistress, and while the two stories have many different features, they have some curiously alike. In one case she flees from her mistress before

the birth of her son (Gen. xvi. 6 ff.), while in the other she is
expelled at the wish of her mistress some years later (Gen.
xxi. 9 ff.) but in both the story culminates in an incident that
takes place near a well in the wilderness, and in both there is an
angelic visitation and a promise of greatness for Ishmael. While
there is no impossibility in supposing that these were all
duplicated incidents, this is of varying improbability, and it is
easier to suppose that we have alternative traditions of single
incidents.

(3) More serious are the cases of actual disagreement in the
narratives of the Pentateuch. Sometimes these are found in
separate narratives that lie side by side, and sometimes within
what appears to be a single narrative. The first two chapters of
the Bible contain two irreconcilable accounts of the Creation.
According to the first account man and woman were created
together as the crown and climax of creation, after all the birds
and animals, whereas according to the second account the
creation of man preceded the creation of the animals and birds
while the creation of woman followed their creation. Again in
the story of the Flood we find that according to Gen. vi. 19 f.
Noah is commanded to take a single pair of every species into
the Ark, whereas according to Gen. vii. 2 he is bidden to take
seven pairs of clean beasts and a single pair of the unclean.
Gen. vii. 8 f. emphasizes this contradiction with its specific
statement that of clean and unclean a single pair went into the
Ark, though it is possible that the emphasis on the contradiction
is not original. Similarly there is disagreement in the duration
of the Flood. According to Gen. vii. 12 the rains lasted forty
days, after which, according to viii. 6 ff., Noah waited for
certain periods of seven days before the waters were abated,
whereas according to Gen. vii. 24 the waters prevailed for a
hundred and fifty days, and were not finally abated until a year
and ten days after the beginning of the Flood (viii. 14; cf. vii.
11).

In Gen. xxxvii. 27 Judah proposes that Joseph should be
sold to some Ishmaelites, and the following verse states that this
was done, while Gen. xxxix. 1 says the Ishmaelites sold him to
an Egyptian. But Gen. xxxvii. 28a introduces Midianites who
passed by and kidnapped Joseph from the pit, without the

knowledge of his brethren (29 f.), and who later sold Joseph to
Potiphar (xxxvii. 36).

In Exod. xxv–xxxi Moses receives instructions on the sacred
mount for the construction of the Tabernacle, and in Exod.
xxxv–xl we read that he passed on the instructions, and the
Tabernacle was actually made. This Tabernacle was a very
elaborate structure, and its custodians were the Levites, num-
bering more than eight thousand (Num. i. 49–53, iii, iv). It was
always located in the centre of the camp in resting, and also in
the centre of the Israelite tribes in travelling (Num. ii). Between
the issue of the instructions for the making of this Tabernacle
and its actual construction, we read of another and simpler
Tent (Exod. xxxiii. 7–11). This stood outside the camp and
afar off, and was kept by a single attendant, Joshua, an Ephraimite. It cannot be supposed that this was for temporary use,
until the other was prepared, since it figures in the story later
(Num. xi. 16 ff., xii. 4 ff.), and it is therefore apparent that it
testifies to a discrepant view of the character and location of
the Tent.

In Num. xiii f. we have the story of the sending of the
spies into the Promised Land. We read that they went to
Hebron (xiii. 22), and brought back a report of the fertility of
the land (xiii. 27, xiv. 8 f.), but that all save Caleb discouraged
the people (xiii. 30 f.) and that Caleb alone was promised
admission to the land (xiv. 24). Yet interspersed with this we
read that the spies went through the whole length of the land to
Rehob (xiii. 21), and reported that it was "a land that eateth up
its inhabitants" (xiii. 32), and that two spies, Joshua and Caleb,
presented the minority report (xiv. 6 f.) and were promised
exemption from the punishment pronounced on the people
(xiv. 30). It is therefore apparent that here again there are
discrepant details.

In Gen. xxvii we find Isaac lying on his death bed, and
Jacob's departure for Paddan-aram is represented as arising out
of the incident there recorded. Yet according to the chronology
of the book Isaac must have spent eighty years on his death
bed (cf. Gen. xxv. 26, xxvi. 34, xxxv. 28). By supposing that
Rebekah only began to get anxious lest Jacob should follow his
brother's example some thirty-seven years after Esau married

Hittite wives, when Jacob was now seventy-seven years old, Keil proposed to reduce the duration of Isaac's last illness to forty-three years. But this harmonizing effort only provides eloquent testimony to the intractableness of the difficulty.

(4) In the laws of the Pentateuch disagreements and inconsistencies are also found. In Exod. xx. 24 it is laid down that an altar is to be set up in every place which the Lord should appoint, whereas in Deut. xii. 14 it is forbidden to offer sacrifice except at a single legitimate sanctuary. The offering of sacrifices is reserved for the descendants of Aaron, according to Exod. xxviii. 1, but open to any member of the Levite tribe, according to Deut. xviii. 7. The duration of the Feast of Tabernacles is seven days, according to Deut. xvi. 15, but eight days, according to Lev. xxiii. 36.

The law of sanctuary is found in various forms. In Exod. xxi. 12 ff. the unintentional homicide is granted the asylum of the altar. Deut. xix. 1–13 and Num. xxxv. 9–24 do not mention the altar, but specify a number of cities in which he may find asylum. The former passage commands that three such cities shall be set aside, but provides that three others may be added if Israel's borders are enlarged, while the latter passage, attributed to a date some months earlier than the other, already provides for six cities.

In Exod. xxi. 2 ff. it is laid down that a Hebrew male slave must be released after six years of servitude, but it is specifically stated that a female slave is not similarly entitled to release. In disagreement with this Deut. xv. 12 places both male and female slaves on the same footing in this respect.

(5) Discrepant statements are found in relation to the Divine name. It is sometimes supposed that this is the chief, or even the only, basis of Pentateuchal criticism, and that if it can be shown that the two terms for the Divine Being have sometimes been confused in the transmission of the text, the whole case falls. Elaborate efforts are sometimes made to show why a writer who was familiar with both terms may have used now the one and now the other for definite reasons. All this ignores the flat contradictions contained in the text.

Exod. vi. 2 f. says: "I am Jehovah, and I appeared unto Abraham, unto Isaac, and unto Jacob as El Shaddai, but *by my name Jehovah I was not known to them.*" Yet there are several passages in the book of Genesis which declare that God *was* known to the patriarchs by the name Jehovah. The name is known to Abram (Gen. xv. 2, 8) to Sarai (xvi. 2), to Laban (xxiv. 31); it is used by angelic visitors in conversation with Abraham (xviii. 14) and with Lot (xix. 13); and *God is represented as saying "I am Jehovah"* to Abram (xv. 7) and to Jacob (xxviii. 13). There are even passages which carry the use of this Divine name far back beyond the patriarchs. Gen. iv. 26 states that in the days of Seth, the son of Adam, men began to call on the name of Jehovah, and Gen. iv. 1 says that even before this Jehovah's name was found on the lips of Eve in the moment when she first became a mother.

(6) Between the first and second accounts of the Creation there is a difference in the conception of God. In the second account we find a naïve anthropomorphism. Jehovah is represented as moulding man from the dust and breathing into his nostrils (Gen. ii. 7), as building woman from a rib which He has taken from the man (ii. 22), after a series of experiments to find a suitable partner for the man (ii. 18–20), as planting a garden (ii. 8), and later taking a walk in it in the cool of the day (iii. 8). In the first account there is none of this. God is a Being of transcendent dignity and power, whose word suffices to effect its own fulfilment. He says "Let us make man in our image" (Gen. i. 26), but it is improbable that even there the thought is of man's physical likeness to God. For man is distinguished from the animal world not by the difference of his bodily form, but by spiritual qualities which enable him to have dominion over the animal world. It is in these fundamental differentiae that the image of God is to be found, and in harmony with this the chapter nowhere attributes to God bodily actions.

His command brings all things into being, and He is aware of this without the necessity to take a journey. This contrasts with the walk in the Garden of Eden, and the search for the hiding Adam and Eve. It also contrasts with other passages we find later. In the story of Noah, the simple anthropomorphism reappears when Jehovah shuts Noah in the Ark (vii. 16), and when He smells the sweet savour of Noah's sacrifice (viii. 21).

Similarly, in the story of the tower of Babel, Jehovah has to come down to see what is going on (xi. 5). It is also to be noted that there are a number of passages which represent an attitude intermediate between these two. They do not picture God as appearing amongst men in human form, but as sending an angelic representative in human form to convey His message (Gen. xxi. 17, xxii. 11, xxviii. 12, xxxi. 11, xxxii. 1), or as appearing to men in dreams (Gen. xx. 3, xxviii. 12, xxxi. 24).

(7) There are marked differences of style in various parts of the Pentateuch. The book of Deuteronomy is characterized by a rhetorical and hortatory style, and by a whole series of oft-repeated phrases. Other parts of the Pentateuch, scattered through the first four books, have a dry and formal style, marked again by many characteristic expressions, and by frequent repetition. There are yet other passages whose simple and artless style reveals the unsurpassed art of the story-teller.

It is sometimes supposed that these differences may be accounted for merely by the difference of subject-matter in the different parts of the Pentateuch. A modern lawyer, who can employ legal phraseology in drafting a legal document, would not employ the same style in his private correspondence, or in a volume of essays. Similarly, when we find one style in narrative, another in public oration, and yet another in legal and ritual regulations, we need not assume a multiplicity of authors. In fact, however, the case is not quite so simple as this. The varieties of style can be found in passages that lie beside one another, where the subject matter is the same, and where the general character of the passage cannot be sharply distinguished in this way. A single writer may have variety of expression for a single idea, and the mere fact that we now find "male and female" and now "man and woman" would by itself have no significance. But what we find is a whole series of alternative expressions for common ideas, and *each set belongs together*.

From these various lines of approach we soon find that we reach converging results. The exalted and transcendent view of God is found to be associated with the dry and repetitious style, and the name Jehovah does not figure prior to the revelation to Moses where this style is found. On the other hand the simple

and artless narrative provides us with the naïve anthropomorphism, and commonly uses the name Jehovah from the beginning
of the story. Many of the inconsistencies and discrepancies
now resolve themselves, and we find a general inner consistency
between the groups of narratives we secure. Some of the doublets also sort themselves out, and we find that the one belongs to
this group and the other to that. Yet some perplexities remain.
For if we use the clue of style we find that amongst the simple
narratives there are still some doublets, and the Divine name
is sometimes Jehovah and sometimes God in Genesis, while if
we use the clue of the Divine names we find that two distinguishable styles are found together, and almost all the passages
about dreams and angels are found alongside those which
present the transcendent view of God.

This leads to the conclusion that there are at least three
collections of material found in the Pentateuch, apart from the
bulk of the book of Deuteronomy, which yields a separate
block, whose style is almost entirely absent from the rest of the
Pentateuch. The third of these three shares with the formal and
repetitious collection the view that the name Jehovah was not
known to Israel before the time of Moses, but shares with the
other collection its simple and artless style. Closer examination
reveals some stylistic characteristics, but the test of style is very
hard to apply as between the two groups of simple narratives.
We find that most of the remaining doublets now sort themselves
out, and also that our third source shows some characteristic
interests. For practically all the references to dreams and angels
belong to it.

No one of these clues can be applied throughout the whole
of the Pentateuch. However strongly marked a writer's style, it
does not reveal itself in every sentence he writes. Ruskin and
Carlyle have easily distinguishable styles, but it would be easy
to find individual sentences of either which could not be
immediately identified by their style alone. Where there are
continuous passages in the Pentateuch, the collection to which
they belong can be identified, but where two of the collections
deal with a common theme, and material from both has been
interwoven, it is not always easy to delimit with exactness by
the test of style alone where the joins occur. But where two or

more of our clues overlap we find that they reinforce and confirm one another.

For instance, between the two accounts of the Creation there is a disagreement as to the sequence of creation, a difference in the usage of the divine names, a difference in the conception of God, and a difference of style. And wherever two or more of the tests are applicable we find they support one another. We are therefore able to trust them where only one is found, and so to follow now this and now that, according as it appears in the particular narrative or verse. Many writers try to carry the exact delimitation of the various collections throughout the whole of the Pentateuch, and to assign every verse or part of a verse to its appropriate source. That they often disagree in the precise delimitation is not surprising. But the real significance of Pentateuchal criticism is not to be found in its ability to do this, but in its demonstration that the Pentateuch contains material from these different collections, and in its study of the character, outlook and date of these collections.

To us it may seem strange that an author should use two different accounts of the same event, and weave them together into a single narrative, but we have clear evidence of the methods of ancient writers. Many writers have referred to Tatian, who took the four Gospels, and wove them into a continuous narrative in his Diatessaron, using the actual words of Scripture, and passing from one account to another freely. New Testament scholars have shown that the authors of the First and Third Gospels used Mark and a lost document called Q, and extracted material from them, but each in his own way, and each altering what he incorporated as he thought fit.

A study of the books of Kings and Chronicles is one of the most revealing and rewarding the student of ancient literary methods can undertake. It is soon obvious that the books of Kings formed one of the sources of the Chronicler, but not his only source. Sometimes he copied passages verbatim from his source, perhaps altering an occasional word, or slightly abbreviating; sometimes he made important alterations clearly dictated by his own presuppositions, or his own ideas of propriety. Where he is resting on other sources it is therefore probable that his method is the same.

We need not, therefore, be surprised that the compiler of the Pentateuch should have extracted material from older sources, or should have worked material from more than one source into a continuous narrative, or should have felt himself free to make slight alterations in what he took over, or have composed the joins in his narratives. These alterations and joins are usually attributed to the Redactor, and it should occasion no surprise that the compiler or redactor has left some traces of his own work.

The main sources of the Pentateuch already referred to are usually called by the letters J, E, D, and P. Their characters and contents may be briefly indicated before we turn to the question of their order and date.

The symbol J stands for Jehovistic, and it indicates that this is the source which ascribes the use of the name Jehovah[1] to primeval times. It begins with the second account of the Creation, and is marked by that naïve anthropomorphism already noted. Its style is simple, but brilliantly effective, and the literary genius of its author will make it live, if only as literature, so long as men read literature. Angels are not characteristic of this source, though they figure occasionally in it. It has a special interest in the south. Abraham's residence is in Hebron, and it is to Hebron that the spies go. In the Joseph story it is Judah who takes the lead. Hence the symbol J serves also to mark it as the Judahite document or collection.

The symbol E stands for Elohistic, and it indicates that this source uses Elohim, or God, for the Divine Being prior to the Mosaic revelation—though this feature the E document has in common with P. E begins with the patriarch Abraham, and not with the Creation. It is the source that has a special interest in dreams and angels, and its anthropomorphism is not so naïve as J's. It has a fondness for scenes of blessing and of farewell. It has a special interest in the northern tribes, and since Ephraim was the most important of those tribes, the symbol E serves to mark it as the Ephraimite source. In the Joseph story it is here

[1] This word is really a hybrid, formed of the consonants of the Divine name, probably pronounced Yahweh, and the vowels of the word Adonai = Lord. The form Jehovah is retained in the present book, however, as the more familiar if less accurate form. There can, indeed, be no final certainty as to what the vowels of YHWH really were.

Reuben who takes the lead, and the Ephraimite Joshua has special prominence in the period of the Exodus. In the Jacob story Bethel and Shechem are the centres of its interest. In the Abraham story Beersheba enjoys the position of prominence, but though this was situated in the far south, this is not inconsistent with an interest in the northern tribes, since as late as the period of Amos northern tribesmen went on pilgrimage to Beersheba (cf. Amos v. 5, viii. 14).

Both J and E depict the patriarchs as worshipping and sacrificing by sacred stones and wells and trees, and neither knows any need of priests to offer the sacrifices. It has been already said that the style of these two sources is very similar and their delimitation is sometimes very difficult where their special features are not found. It is common to use the symbol JE for passages which cannot be precisely analysed as between these sources. The section of laws, known as the Book of the Covenant, which is found in Exod. xx. 22 to xxiii. 33, is commonly ascribed to JE, but regarded as predominantly from E. It may well have been incorporated from an originally independent source. It is preceded by the Decalogue, which originally consisted wholly of short words, similar to those which mark the second part. Some of the earlier words have been much expanded, and there are marks of P in the present expansion of Exod. xx. In its original short form the Decalogue is doubtless very ancient, and there is no reason to doubt that it was given to Israel through Moses. The book of the Covenant is a commentary on the Decalogue, giving examples of the application of its principles, and it is probable that it dates from an early period, earlier than that of the J and E documents, but has had some editorial revision.

The symbol D stands for Deuteronomy, and it indicates that this is the source which is almost exclusively limited to that book, and which occupies almost the whole of that book. Its earlier part consists of a historical retrospect, interspersed with exhortation, and from chapter xii it sets forth the Deuteronomic Code of Laws. Its dominant interest is in the purity of the religion of Israel, and it limits the offering of sacrifice to one legitimate sanctuary, and the custody of the ritual to the tribe of Levi. It knows of no distinctions within that tribe, however, but

admits all its members to the service of the altar. It is strongly
opposed to all Canaanite religious rites and symbols. It is
marked by its humanitarian interest, and frequently commends
the needy classes to the care of men. Amongst the needy classes
the Levites figure conspicuously. The pragmatism of the book
is also to be noted. It teaches that the fortunes of Israel will
inevitably reflect its religious loyalty, and that when it is faithful
and pure in its worship and life, prosperity will mark its way,
while religious declension will be followed by disaster and
curse.

The symbol P stands for the Priestly Code, and it indicates
that this document contains the bulk of the regulations for the
sacrificial cultus and the ordering of the priesthood. It begins
with the first account of the Creation, and it has a great fondness
for genealogies. Its view of God is the most transcendent in the
Pentateuch, and its style is the formal and repetitious one, to
which reference has been made. It attributes the first revelation
of the name Jehovah to Israel as made to Moses. With a single
exception it knows nothing of theophanies. That exception was
connected with Bethel (Gen. xxxv. 9 ff.), and it can only be
conjectured why this survived. It records no sacrifices prior
to the time of Moses and Aaron, and it is probable that this is
because it could not recognize the legitimacy of sacrifice until
it had been divinely established, and unless it was offered by the
duly appointed priests. It draws a distinction between the
descendants of Aaron, who alone are authorized to offer sacrifices, and the rest of the tribe of Levi, to whom the more menial
duties of the sacred service are assigned. It makes elaborate
provisions for the maintenance of priests and Levites, and
therefore does not commend Levites to the alms of the people.
Nowhere does it contend for the principle of the single legitimate
sanctuary, but it takes it for granted.

Incorporated in P is a section with characteristics of its own,
known by the symbol H, or the Code of Holiness. This is found
in Leviticus xvii to xxvi, and it was probably of independent
origin from P. Its language has some characteristics of its own,
and its concluding verse implies that it brought a collection of
laws to a close. It summons men to holiness with the words
"Ye shall be holy, for I Jehovah your God am holy" (Lev. xix.

2), and frequently reinforces its ordinances with the reminder "I am Jehovah."

What is known as the Graf-Wellhausen theory is merely a theory as to the order of the principal sources above mentioned. The detection of those sources was the work of older scholars, but it was generally held that P was the oldest of the sources until the Graf-Wellhausen school put them in the order J, E, D, P. The reasons for that order are as cogent to-day as ever.

That J and E are older than D, and P younger, is established along three lines. In the first place, D shows knowledge of the historical material of JE, but not of P where P differs. Thus, in the account of the spies in Num. xiii f. it is the JE source which carries the spies only to Eshcol, in the neighbourhood of Hebron, and which exempts Caleb alone from the punishment of exclusion from the promised land, while the P source carries the spies to Rehob in the far north, and exempts Joshua and Caleb. Deut. i. 24, 36 shows knowledge of the former only. Similarly, Num. xvi in its present form deals with two separate and distinct matters, but combined and presented as one. These are the incidents of Dathan and Abiram, and of Korah and his company. The Dathan and Abiram narrative is extracted from JE and the Korah narrative from P. Deut. xi. 6 shows knowledge of the former only.

In the second place, the legal sections of D show a knowledge of the Book of the Covenant, which was incorporated in JE, but no knowledge of P. The laws of the Book of the Covenant are traversed, and sometimes quoted, but nowhere are the provisions of P referred to. The principle of the centralization of the cultus sometimes determines a revision of the older law, and on the question of the priesthood the contribution of D has already been mentioned. As against the absence of any regulation of a priesthood in JE, D provides for a priesthood, but far less elaborately than P. Sometimes the modifications in the law of the Book of the Covenant may reflect the changes which had been introduced by a later age, prior to the codification by the Deuteronomist, but at other times it is more likely that the changes were dictated by his dominant interests in the purity of the religion and the humanity of the conduct of Israel.

In the third place, the history as recorded in the surviving historical books shows that the multiplicity of altars permitted by the Book of the Covenant continued down to the time of Hezekiah, without any awareness of wrongdoing. Elijah complained that Jehovah's altars had been demolished (1 Kings xix. 10) and himself rebuilt one on Carmel (1 Kings xviii. 30) with divine approval. The practice of sanctuary at the beginning of Solomon's reign was in accordance with the Book of the Covenant, and not in accordance with the law of either D or P. Before the Exile there is no betrayal of any knowledge of the provision of P. The books of Kings, which appear to have been compiled in the sixth century B.C., view all the history from the Deuteronomic point of view, but the compilers do not seem to have known P. On the other hand, the Chronicler knew P, and re-wrote some of the history to bring it into accord with it. He changed the Carian or Cherethite mercenaries of 2 Kings xi. 4 into Levites (2 Chron. xxiii. 2 ff.), since the foreign mercenaries should not have been admitted to the sacred enclosure by the law of P. He explained the death of Uzzah by the fact that he was not a Levite (1 Chron. xv. 13), though the earlier 2 Sam. vi knows nothing of this explanation in terms of the laws of P.

The Code of Deuteronomy is therefore of vital importance in Pentateuchal criticism, since it is primarily by relation to it that the other documents are dated. Moreover, that Code can be more precisely dated with a greater measure of probability than any other. For it is in the highest degree probable that the Law Book on which Josiah's reform was based was the book of Deuteronomy, and that the book first became publicly known at that time.

In the narrative of Josiah's reform we read that the priest Hilkiah found a law-book in the Temple in the eighteenth year of the king (621 B.C.), when the Temple was being repaired (2 Kings xxii. 8), and on the basis of this book the reform was carried through. The principal features of the reform were the centralization of worship and sacrifice, and the abolition of all the provincial shrines. All images, and cultic objects associated with the old Canaanite sanctuaries, sacred pillars and posts (*mazzēbōth* and *ashērīm*), were destroyed, and all sacred

prostitution was done away with, and when in the following
year the feast of the Passover was observed, it was centralized
in Jerusalem. Every one of these reforms could find its basis in
the book of Deuteronomy, and there is no reason to look beyond
this book for their inspiration. When the law-book was read
before the king, he was alarmed at the curse it pronounced
on those who did not carry out its provisions, and again
Deuteronomy xxviii. 15–68 can provide the appropriate basis
for his fear.

In one respect only the reform did not implement the provisions of Deuteronomy, and the account in 2 Kings draws
special attention to this, and thus indicates that there was
reason to expect its implementation. It notes that the country
priests did not come to minister in Jerusalem (2 Kings xxiii. 9),
and so even here points to Deut. xviii. 6 ff. As it is unlikely
that Josiah's law-book was the whole Pentateuch, and as there is
no reason to look beyond Deuteronomy for its known features,
it has long been believed that it is to be found in the book of
Deuteronomy. Probably it was not the whole of the present
book, however. The introductory discourse to the Code proper is
found in chapters v–xi, and the Code itself in chapters xii–xxvi,
and xxviii, and it is probable that Josiah's law-book contained
no more than this. Chapters i–iv are a second and independent
introduction, though written by a writer of the same school as
the main work, while the closing chapters of the book are more
miscellaneous.

Many writers believe that the Code of Deuteronomy was
written immediately before the Reform, and that its finding by
Hilkiah was but make-believe. This seems in the highest degree
improbable. For if the Jerusalem priestly circles of that day had
prepared this Code specifically for the reform, they would
hardly have included the provision for the country priests to
share their privileges, whose implementation they successfully
resisted. There is no reason to doubt that it had lain for many
years in the Temple, and was genuinely found. Sellin, whose
latest view is that the book was written immediately prior to the
reform, formerly held that it was written before Hezekiah's
reform, and formed the basis of his reform. This seems to err
as much in the other direction. We read in 2 Kings xviii of

that the provisions of P were those that were followed in the Jewish community at the beginning of the Christian era.

It should be observed that the assignment of P to the post-exilic age does not mean that it is supposed that all the ritual practices laid down in P are of post-exilic invention. The codification of law does not mean the rejection of everything older than the codification. It involves some changes in the harmonizing of the regulations codified, and if the codification is undertaken under the influence of some new principle, such as D's principle of the centralization of the cultus, then it will involve major changes where that principle dictates. But elsewhere it gathers into itself regulations and practices that may be very ancient. It is often pointed out in recent years that we now have evidence in the Ras Shamra texts that some of the types of sacrifice that do not figure in JE or D, but only in P in the Old Testament, were already found at Ras Shamra in the fourteenth century B.C. This may, or may not, mean that they belonged to Israelite practice all down the years. For the compromise that brought others than the Jerusalem Zadokites into the recognized priesthood may well have brought practices from some other shrines into the new official corpus of rituals.

What the Priestly Code sought to do was to regulate the ritual, and to ensure that all permitted practices were related to the purest worship of Jehovah, and purged of every taint of the things that Deuteronomy had denounced. For P is concerned with the purity of the worship no less than D. But whereas D sought to eliminate the multiplicity of shrines and to centralize the worship in one sanctuary, P carried this work further by codifying the ritual of that sanctuary. Neither JE nor D had attempted to do this, and all that we can say is that this codification comes from the post-exilic age, and not that everything here codified is of post-exilic origin. This distinction should be kept clearly in mind.

The first promulgation of the law of P would seem to have been made by Ezra. He came to Jerusalem with the law of God in his hand (Ezra vii. 14), and there publicly read it and established it (Neh. viii). That his law at least contained P is apparent from the fact that its Feast of Tabernacles was an

Hezekiah's reform, which also consisted in a centralization of the cultus. Some writers have cast doubt on this as an anticipation of Josiah's reform. But there is every reason to believe that Hezekiah did carry through a reform of religion, and none to doubt that he attempted its centralization. But since no law-book is even hinted at in connexion with his reform, there is no reason to suppose that it was based on one.

It is probable, therefore, that the book of Deuteronomy was written between these two reforms, and that it embodied the lessons of the failure of the one, and prepared a programme which was acted on in the other. The reign of Manasseh was a time of reaction, and the reforming circles might be expected to be laying their plans for a further attempt at reform. Probably the experience in Hezekiah's time had made them aware of the problems that had to be overcome. For instance, hitherto all slaughter had been sacrifice. But the limitation of sacrifice to a single shrine would make impracticable the bringing thither of animals from all parts of the land. Hence Deuteronomy provided for slaughter for food to take place anywhere (Deut. xii. 20 ff.).

Again, the closing of the local shrines would mean the loss of the livelihood of the local priests. Hence Deuteronomy commended them to the generosity of the people they had hitherto served, and also provided that they should be entitled to continue to act for them on the occasions when they went up to the sacred shrine (Deut. xviii. 6 ff.). But plans for reform in the reign of Manasseh were dangerous (2 Kings xxi. 16), and whoever prepared Deuteronomy in that reign would have to keep it secret. And since the reign of Manasseh lasted fifty-five years, the plan would long have been forgotten before it could be put into effect, and the people who prepared it long have died before the eighteenth year of Josiah, so that when it was discovered in the Temple no one living knew where it had come from or what was its age. Hence we may date the compilation of Deuteronomy *circa* 680 B.C. and its promulgation 621 B.C.

How much older than D the documents J and E are is a more difficult question. Both J and E are corpora of traditions of all the tribes, and not merely of the southern and the northern tribes respectively, and they are not likely to have been made before the early days of the monarchy when Judah first came into the stream of a common life with the northern tribes. In that age there would be a bringing together of the various traditions and imposing upon them of a unity that would reflect the existing unity of the tribes. Yet it is probable that J and E in their present form date from after the Disruption. We know that despite the Disruption both north and south still cherished the ideal of unity, and the differing points of view of J and E in presenting the united traditions of the tribes could well come from an age in which the two parts of the land stood in rivalry, each believing it was the real repository of the traditions.

The J source is generally believed to have been drawn on by the compiler of the book of Joshua, and to have contained the poetic citation of Joshua x. 13 from the Book of Jashar. Since the Book of Jashar contained David's Lament for Saul and Jonathan (2 Sam. i. 18) it cannot have been compiled before David's reign, and hence J cannot well be earlier than this. Again, the form of the blessing of Gen. xv. 18 appears to reflect the boundaries of Solomon's kingdom (1 Kings iv. 21), so that again we are pointed to about the same age for the *terminus a quo* for J. There is no reason to carry it down very far beyond the age of Solomon in the post-Disruption age, and a date 900 to 850 B.C. would seem to satisfy the conditions. Many scholars place it nearer to the latter date on the ground that Joshua vi. 26 appears to reflect the incident recorded in 1 Kings xvi. 34, which took place in the reign of Ahab.

Since J is more primitive in character than E, it is generally believed that E is younger than J. It is thought that Joseph's dreams reflect the sovereignty of the house of Ephraim, and the oracles of Balaam, which were incorporated in E, are believed to reflect a period of Israelite prosperity. No great cogency can be attributed to these arguments, and in particular it is probable that the Balaam oracles are much older than the E document in which they were incorporated. That the E document comes from the period 800 to 750 B.C. is probable, though we have only slight indications of this, and we ought not to number amongst them the prosperity of the reign of Jeroboam II as providing the background of the Balaam oracles. The covenant of Gen. xxxi.

44 ff. would seem to indicate that the period of the Syri is past, and so would carry us to a date not earlier tha 800 B.C., while if the E document is of northern origin it dated before the fall of Samaria (721 B.C.), and probably the dark and unsettled quarter of a century that preced fall.

The date of P is carried into the post-exilic age if it than Deuteronomy, which was promulgated less than years before the Exile. It will be seen later that D don the historical books compiled during the sixth centur and there is no serious influence of P upon them. Mo P would appear to be later than the book of Ezekiel. Fo book both rationalizes the failure of the country prie secure an equal place beside the Jerusalem priests, and poses a compromise. Instead of equating the terms and priest, as the book of Deuteronomy does, Ezek. xli ff., 15 ff. distinguishes between the Levites of the co shrines and the Jerusalem Levites, the sons of Zadok. I restored community the former are to have a lower s than the latter as the punishment for the idolatry that on in their shrines. Nevertheless, they are assigned duti the Temple, though not the priestly office.

In P, however, we find the priestly office assigned wider body than the old Jerusalem priesthood, the Zadol It is assigned to all descendants of Aaron, of whom the Z kites were reckoned but a part. The rest of the Levites assigned the lower duties in the Temple, but there i suggestion that this is a punishment for things that took in the pre-exilic days. It is represented as a divine ordina going back to the days of Moses. It is quite clear that writer of Ezek. xliv, who was either the sixth century pro Ezekiel or a disciple of his writing shortly after his time, unaware of the provisions of P, and equally clear that chapter provides an intermediate stage of the developm from the law of D to that of P. The compromise there posed was substantially adopted, but with some modifica in the extension of the priestly section of the Levites. older view that P was the oldest of the sources of the Pe teuch is therefore no longer held, and especially as we kr

eight days feast (Neh. viii. 18), in agreement with P's (Lev. xxiii. 36), as against D's (Deut. xvi. 13). Moreover, its Temple tax (Neh. x. 32), is enjoined only in P (Exod. xxx. 13), though its amount in P is somewhat larger than in Ezra's time. If Ezra's law included the whole of the Pentateuch, we are without knowledge of any occasion between the date of Ezekiel's sketch of the future community and Ezra's time when P could have been issued. It is more likely that this notable occasion saw the issue of a new code than that the new code had appeared on an unrecorded occasion, and that Ezra brought nothing specially new with him.

On the other hand, the combination of the new law of P with the older parts of the Pentateuch must have followed swiftly on the work of Ezra, since the Samaritans recognize the whole of the Pentateuch, and are not likely to have taken it over after their breach with the Jews. Of the precise date of that breach we have less specific information than we could wish. The days of Nehemiah saw some stages in its development, but it is probable that it did not become definite and complete until some time in the fourth century B.C. The date of Ezra's promulgation of the law of P has commonly been held to be 444 B.C., but in modern times many scholars have believed, for reasons that will be given below, that it was in 397 B.C.

Reference has been made to the Holiness Code that was embodied in P. That it is older than P is generally agreed, and it seems to have some affinities with Ezekiel. But of its date relative to that of D there is no agreement, and some scholars think it is slightly earlier than D and others that it is rather later. In fact it would seem to be entirely independent of D, and to have issued from quite separate circles from D, and there is therefore no means of determining their relative date. If one were prepared with the other before it, in order to correct or modify the other, their relative date would be a profitable study. But if they were quite independent of one another the position is different. H specifically forbids secular slaughter (Lev. xvii. 3 f.), whereas it has been already said that D permits it.

Oesterley and Robinson find it hard to believe that this

could have been written after the appearance of D, though it would be just as easy to suppose that the very emphasis of its rejection of secular slaughter was due to some recent challenge to the hitherto invariable rule that all slaughter must be sacrificial. It has to be remembered that Josiah's centralization of worship did not last, and with the reopening of other shrines the necessity for D's change in this matter lapsed. H was concerned to attack the problem of religious impurity in another way, by the regulation of the ritual and by the evoking of the spirit of loyalty. P combined the two, accepting and taking for granted D's principle of centralization, and carrying through the regulation of the ritual begun in H and Ezek. xl–xlviii. The present writer would place H in the sixth century B.C.

Of the actual process of the compilation of the Pentateuch we have no record. It is probable that J and E had already been combined before D was prepared. With the collapse of the northern kingdom and its monarchy, the southern kingdom would become the centre of the hopes of the nation, and Josiah's reform seems to have gone beyond the limits of the southern kingdom. It should be remembered that his reform was the religious side of a bid for independence on the occasion of the approaching collapse of the Assyrian empire, and it would be natural to expect that the northern kingdom as well as Judah would welcome deliverance from the Assyrian yoke, and would accept Judah's leadership in such a cause. This may explain why the group that planned the Deuteronomic reform early in Manasseh's reign, little more than a quarter of a century after the fall of the northern kingdom, were at pains to embody northern features in their programme. For D has many northern connexions, as has been emphasized in recent years. If their purpose was to mobilize north and south in a new national unity they could be understood.

When J and E were combined, it would be inevitable that joins would be made by the compiler, and if D were subsequently added the new compiler might be expected to show signs of his hand, though slighter since the material of JE and D was not interspersed. Later P was taken and made the groundwork of the completed Pentateuch, material from JED being fitted into a

framework of P, with joins and minor modifications once more
revealing the editorial hand of the compiler.

(b) The Sources Behind the Sources

It is not to be supposed that any of these main sources of
the Pentateuch is a simple and uniform document, written out
of the head of a single writer. That even the oldest of the sources
J and E rest on older traditions has already been said, and
while it is probable that those traditions were first brought
together in the period of the united Monarchy, the individual
traditions were probably much older. Nor need we suppose
that the compilers of J and E rested only on oral sources.
Indeed it is quite certain that they used older literary sources.
For we find embedded in the Pentateuch a number of passages,
mainly in poetry, cited from elsewhere. Many of these were
cited in the principal documents of the Pentateuch, but others
cannot be ascribed with confidence to any of the documents,
and may have been independently incorporated. This means
that there is reason to suppose that there were very ancient
written sources dealing with the period covered by the Pentateuch.

The poetic material in the Pentateuch is of various types.
Some of it may perhaps have been cited from oral sources, but
that some of it was from written sources is specifically stated,
and it is likely that many passages whose written source is not
indicated were taken from such a source.

(1) There are several fragments from tribal and local
songs. Of these we may note:

(i) The song of Lamech (Gen. iv. 23 f.). This ancient song of
the Lamech tribe, breathing out the ferocity on which the tribe
prided itself, has no necessary connexion with the genealogy
that precedes it, and we know neither the source from which
J cites it, nor its age.

(ii) The sites of Moab (Num. xxi. 14 f.). This is a fragment
commencing in the middle of one sentence and breaking off in
the middle of the next, which is chiefly valuable because it is
our only witness to an ancient work, from which it is cited, the

Book of the Wars of Jehovah. It was probably E which preserved this excerpt.

(iii) The Song of the Well (Num. xxi. 17 f.). This is a popular snatch, preserved by J or E, whose character is obscured by its setting, which suggests that it is a historical poem.

(iv) The Song of Heshbon and Sihon (Num. xxi. 27 ff.). This is confessedly not cited from a book, but from the lips of the reciters of poems. Of the age of the poem, or of its precise meaning, we are ignorant. It stood most probably in E.

(2) There are several curses and blessings. Here we may note:

(i) The Blessing and Curse of Noah (Gen. ix. 25–27). First a curse is pronounced on Canaan, and then a blessing on Shem and Japhet. Again the age and significance of the verses, and their relation to the verses that precede, are very problematical, but it is probable that J cites them from a source at least as old as the period of David.

(ii) The Blessing of Melchizedek (Gen. xiv. 19 f.) This is found in a chapter which abounds in problems, and which is not usually assigned to any of the major sources of the Pentateuch. It is often assigned to a relatively late date, but it is much more likely that it was very early. It presents Abram in a role quite different from that of any other narrative. It is possible that it is an Israelite adaptation of something older than the Israelite conquest of Jerusalem, and that the purpose of the adaptation was to justify Israelite worship at a Jerusalem shrine. In that case the adaptation may have been made in the time of David. In any case the blessing here does not appear to be older than the narrative in which it stands, but to have been written for its present place in the narrative.

(iii) The Blessing of Rebekah (Gen. xxiv. 60). This fragment, preserved by J, may be an old fragment of tribal poetry. It is included here, because it is presented as a blessing by the editor who preserved it.

(iv) Isaac's Blessing of Jacob (Gen. xxvii. 27 ff.). This tribal blessing, also preserved by J, is clearly older than its context, which presents it as the blessing of Jacob by a father who had forgotten that he had but two sons (cf. v. 29).

(v) Isaac's Curse of Esau (Gen. xxvii. 39 f.). This ambiguous oracle is most probably to be understood with R.V. margin as a curse, and it may well have been taken by the compiler of J from the same source as its companion, with which it clearly belongs, as its verbal connexions show.

(vi) Jacob's Blessing of Joseph's Sons (Gen. xlviii. 15 f.). There is nothing to indicate the age of this oracle, which E preserves, and which may perhaps have been composed for its context (cf. the characteristic interest in angels).

(vii) The Blessing of Jacob (Gen. xlix). This is a much more considerable poem, with oracles on each of the tribes. A double motif runs through the poem, etymological and emblematic, though not uniformly. In some cases both motifs appear and in some neither, while others show one or the other. This would suggest that the separate parts of the chapter come from more than one source, and it is commonly believed that they come from different ages. The Reuben and Simeon-Levi oracles appear to be the oldest, and these are probably of pre-Davidic origin. The tribe of Simeon early disappeared as a separate entity, and we find no mention of it in the Blessing of Moses (Deut. xxxiii). There, too, the priestly function of the Levites appears, while here Levi shares a common curse with Simeon. The Benjamin, Dan and Issachar oracles are also best ascribed to a pre-monarchic age, and it is possible that the Joseph oracle is very ancient, though this is disputed by many. There is no reference here to the division of the Joseph tribe into two, as in the Blessing of Moses. The oracle on Gad may be later than the Song of Deborah (Judges v), since there the tribal name stands as Gilead, though it could still antedate the monarchy. Of several oracles there is nothing to indicate the age, but the Judah oracle seems to presuppose the Davidic kingdom. It is possible that the compiler of J extracted the parts of this poem from various sources and gave it its present form; but it is equally possible that he took it over from his source as it now stands, and that the assembling of its parts was the work of an older editor.

(viii) The Priestly Blessing (Num. vi. 24 ff.). This stands in P, but there is no reason whatever to doubt that it is much older than that document. It may well have been used in pre-exilic times.

(ix) The Ark Formula (Num. x. 35 f.). This very ancient fragment preserves the cries of the people when the Ark was carried into battle and when it was brought back from the battlefield, rather than cries which were originally composed for changes of camping sites. It was preserved by J and its actual age cannot be determined, but it may be as ancient as the practice of carrying the Ark on to the battlefield.

(x) The Balaam Oracles (Num. xxiii f.). The poems here are embedded in a prose narrative, which is commonly distributed between J and E. The age and origin of the poems, however, is quite a different matter. Reacting against earlier suggestions that the poems might be of post-exilic origin, recent writers have tended to recognize their antiquity, and some or all of them have been ascribed to the period of the united monarchy. Albright goes even further, and ascribes all the oracles to the twelfth century, and sees no reason why they may not be the authentic oracles of a North Syrian diviner at the court of Moab.

(xi) The Oracle of Amalek (Num. xxiv. 20). As the text stands this and the two succeeding oracles are attributed to Balaam. But they contain no reference to Moab, and at the most an implicit reference to Israel. They are therefore most probably of independent origin. This brief snatch probably dates from the period of Saul or David, when Amalek had already suffered severely at Israelite hands.

(xii) The Oracle on the Kenites (Num. xxiv. 21 f.). This obscure oracle seems to promise the destruction of the Kenites by the Assyrians, but it is possible that the Assyrian reference is not original. Neither date nor meaning can be determined.

(xiii) An obscure oracle, apparently on Assyria (Num. xxiv. 23 f.). This appears to promise Assyria trouble from the maritime power of Cyprus. There is no known situation which would provide the background for this, and it is improbable in itself. Some have interpreted the passage in terms of Alexander's conquest of the Persian empire, but it is unlikely that anything so late as this would have secured a place in the Pentateuch, and it is better to confess ignorance of the significance and the date.

(xiv) The Blessing of Moses (Deut. xxxiii). Here we come

again to a long and important poem, similar in character to Gen. xlix, whose influence it shows in parts. But this is more definitely religious in its tone. That it is later than the earliest parts of Gen. xlix, at any rate, is indicated by the fact that Simeon is unmentioned, while Levi is no longer a secular tribe. In general a period of much greater prosperity for the Israelite tribes is reflected here than in the other poem, though Judah appears to be in a state of isolation and depression. The poem is commonly ascribed to the period of Jeroboam II, but by some to the time of Jeroboam I. Sellin, however, ascribes it to the period of the Judges. The reference to Benjamin (verse 12) is often taken to mean that the Temple should be in her borders. But from the time of the Disruption, Jerusalem was reckoned to Judah, and was its capital. Hence it is improbable that any poem written after the Disruption would at once lament Judah's isolation from the north, and glory in Benjamin's possession of the Temple—when it no longer possessed it! It is possible that the Benjamin oracle refers, not to the Temple, but to the charismatic leader, Saul, whom that tribe supplied, and that this is an indication of date.

(3) There are two miscellaneous oracles, which hardly fit into the foregoing category. These are:

(i) Rebecca's Oracle (Gen. xxv. 23). This brief oracle, which was preserved in J, reflects a period when Edom was subject to Israel, and hence not earlier than the time of David.

(ii) The Oracle on Moses (Num. xii. 6–8). Here is an oracle vindicating Moses against the criticism of Aaron and Miriam. From what source E took it, or what may be its age, we have no means of determining.

(4) There are some national songs or fragments. Here we find:

(i) The Song of Moses and the people at the Red Sea (Exod. xv. 1–19), followed by the Song of Miriam (Exod. xv. 21). The latter is almost identical with the first verse of the other, and it may well be a contemporary song, composed by Miriam, which was subsequently expanded in the longer poem. That it is of much later date is evident from the fact that it treats the journey to Canaan and the establishment of the sanctuary as past events. The Deuteronomic phraseology which it contains, and the implicit idea of a single sanctuary which is found in verse 17, carry us down to a date not earlier than the promulgation of D.

(ii) The oath against Amalek (Exod. xvii. 16). This brief word, which is preserved in E, is probably quite old, and goes back to the time when Amalek was a serious thorn in Israel's side.

(5) There is one long and important lyric poem, viz., the Song of Moses (Deut. xxxii). This may be described as a prophetic psalm, i.e., a psalm embodying a religious message characteristic of the prophets. It clearly comes from a time long subsequent to Moses, since it looks back on the period of the wandering over many generations, and depicts Israel as settled in Canaan, and demoralized by its religion, and in consequence chastised by calamity. In its phraseology, it reminds us of Jeremiah, Ezekiel and Deutero-Isaiah, and hence most scholars assign it to the period of the exile.

Quite apart from all this poetic material, incorporated in the Pentateuch, it may well be that the compilers drew sometimes on material outside the main sources, and reference has been made above to one passage, Gen. xiv, where the prose setting, as well as the poetic fragment it contains, is believed to be quite apart from all the principal sources.

(c) Recent Developments in Pentateuchal Criticism

Durir . the last generation there have been two trends in the further study of the Pentateuch. The one has been in the direction of closer analysis of the sources, and of the study of the sources behind the sources, while the other has been away from the Graf-Wellhausen hypothesis altogether, or in favour of a complete shifting of its moorings.

In J there are some elements that appear to ignore the tradition of the Flood and it has therefore long been usual to distinguish two strands, symbolized by J_1 and J_2, in this document. Some writers have taken the J_1 elements and attached to them some further material, and have treated them as an independent source, earlier than all other sources. This early source Eissfeldt calls L, or the Lay source, while Pfeiffer calls it S, or the Southern source, which he associates with Edom, and Morgenstern K, or the Kenite source.

There are considerable differences in the delimitation of this early source between these writers, as well as in their view of its character and provenance. Eissfeldt dates his L in the time of Elijah (i.e., practically the date of J in the view of most scholars), and differentiates it from J much more sharply than most differentiate J_1 from J_2. He believes it was governed by the primitive nomadic ideal, and the desire to protest against the Canaanizing of life. In contrast to this he finds that J rejoices in Canaan and in all its settled life. He then dates J in the first half of the eighth century (i.e., about the time usually assigned to E), and E at the end of the eighth century. Morgenstern dates his K about 900 B.C. and holds that it contained the story of Moses and the settlement of the Israelite tribes and their Kenite allies in the south of Palestine. Amongst its material he finds the ritual Decalogue of Exod. xxxiv, in its original form. Pfeiffer dates his S to the tenth century B.C., but without pinning himself at all precisely to this date. Like Eissfeldt he finds much more of the material of Genesis to belong to this early source than Morgenstern does to his K.

In a similar way von Rad has examined the P document, and has separated sharply the earlier and the later strands it contains. He therefore holds that this is not a single document, but a combination of two separate documents.

Of a somewhat different character is the work of Mowinckel, who has re-examined the early chapters of Genesis, and who finds in them material from E. It is usually held that E begins with Abraham, and that it contains no story of the pre-Abrahamic period. Mowinckel challenges this view, and carries E back to the beginning. Instead, therefore, of finding a J_1 and a J_2 strand, or an L, S, or K and a J, in addition to P, he finds the three main sources, J, E, and P.

Of minor variations in the dating of the documents we can here take no note. We should, perhaps, note the view of Procksch, however, who carries P back to the pre-exilic period, and who ascribes J to the period of Solomon. More important have been the attacks on the normal dating of the promulgation of Deuteronomy, since this is of fundamental importance to the whole critical view. These attacks have been from two sides.

Kennett argued that Deuteronomy was not Josiah's law-book, but that it was of post-exilic origin. The same view was advocated on the continent by Hölscher, who ascribed J to 900 B.C., E to the middle of the sixth century B.C. (i.e., to the period of the exile), D to *circa* 500 B.C., Ezekiel to the fifth century B.C., and P to a yet later date. The chief ground of this attack is the impracticable idealism of D. It is said that it was quite impossible to centralize the observance of the festivals in Jerusalem, or to implement the law of the remission of debt in the seventh year, or the manumission of slaves. Moreover, the account of Josiah's reform given in the Second Book of Kings is held to be unhistorical. Against this it is replied that while Deuteronomy is certainly in some respects an ideal programme, it would have been no less so after the exile than before. Moreover, there is no real ground for questioning the historical character of Josiah's reform, save the theory in whose way it stands.

From the opposite side Oestreicher on the continent, and Welch in this country, have argued that Deuteronomy is much older than has been supposed. Oestreicher claimed that it demanded the purity of the cult, rather than its unity (*nicht Kulteinheit sondern Kultreinheit*), and Welch renewed the same claim. He argued that the book in its original form made no demand for the centralization of the cult, but in order to support this position he was compelled to hold that Deut. xii. 1–7 did not belong to the original book. He dates the book in the early days of the monarchy, and observes that many of its laws are obviously older than the seventh century. This is not in dispute. Any re-codification of British Law to-day would incorporate the provisions of Magna Carta and Habeas Corpus, and in the same way a seventh century re-codification of Israelite law would naturally embody many old laws. Moreover, the fact that the demand for centralization stands at the very beginning of the Code part of Deuteronomy must be given very great weight until the strongest reasons are provided for eliminating it.

Robertson would go even farther than Welch. He propounds the view that the first four books of the Pentateuch were prepared at the time of the foundation of the monarchy from the materials supplied from the various local shrines, and that Deuteronomy was prepared by a committee presided over by Samuel in preparation for the centralization of the cult, which was planned then but not carried through until the time of Solomon. This does not explain why Deuteronomy shows knowledge of the J and E parts of the first four books, both in history and legislation, but not of the P part, and it assumes a centralizing purpose on the part of Samuel and achievement on the part of Solomon that is without any foundation of evidence.

Challenges of a different kind must next be recorded. In 1924 Löhr discussed the Priestly Code in Genesis, and argued that there never was such an independent source as P. He ascribed the Pentateuch to Ezra and his associates, and held that they had before them small groups of narratives, rather than continuous documents. While he held that some of these materials had been worked up into small cycles of narratives, he held that the Pentateuch was the literary creation of one man and his associates. In this he has something in common with Robertson, though he places its composition in a very different age. Löhr found a genuine Mosaic core in Deuteronomy, including the law of centralization.

More recently Volz and Rudolph have argued that there never was an independent document E. They believe J to have been the basis of the narrative, and much that has hitherto been assigned to E they assign to J. The rest is held to be additions made to J in a subsequent edition. In the first instance their work was limited to Genesis, but Rudolph subsequently extended it to the rest of the Hexateuch. Volz added an appendix to the earlier work, in which he argued that P consists exclusively of legislation, and contained no narrative at all.

It should be noted that some Scandinavian writers, and particularly Engnell, tend to decry all attempts to analyse the Pentateuch into sources. Following Noth they think of Deuteronomy and the Former Prophets (i.e., Joshua to 2 Kings) as a single work, and then hold the first four books of the Bible to form a Tetrateuch which was composed in the post-exilic age, on the basis of oral material rather than written sources, and hold that the compiler imposed upon his materials a unity which derived from his purpose.

A yet different line of approach, applied to the legal sections of the Pentateuch, has been somewhat after the style of the New Testament Form Criticism. This has concerned itself with the differing types of command contained in these sections, where we sometimes find direct commands and prohibitions, sometimes hypothetical cases of varying kinds. Whether these can be traced to different sources, each of which used but a single form, is quite another question.

It will be seen that there is a considerable variety of view in recent years, and it is sometimes supposed that the Graf-Wellhausen view is universally discredited and rejected. That it is widely rejected in whole or in part is doubtless true, but there is no view to put in its place that would not be more widely and emphatically rejected. Few of the rival views have won any adherents at all, while the Graf-Wellhausen view has still a respectable following. Before it can be discarded a view as complete and thoroughgoing, taking account of all the facts and related to the history, will have to be provided. A mere concentration on the acknowledged difficulties of the Graf-Wellhausen view, and then on a selection of points that may seem to give support to a rival view, will not do. For none of the rival views can accommodate so many of the facts, or can escape far more difficulties than the view it seeks to replace. Yet having said this, it remains true that the Graf-Wellhausen view is only a working hypothesis, which can be abandoned with alacrity when a more satisfying view is found, but which cannot with profit be abandoned until then.

BOOK II
THE FORMER PROPHETS

CHAPTER III

THE HEBREW HISTORIAN AND HIS PURPOSE

THE Old Testament contains a good deal of what we should call historical writing, and in our Bibles several books that are frequently referred to as the Historical Books stand together. These are Joshua, Judges, Samuel, Kings, Chronicles, Ezra, Nehemiah and Esther. There is also much narrative writing in the Pentateuch, that embodies the historical traditions of Israel. The historical worth of these works from the modern point of view varies greatly, but the ancient author was not really interested in history from the modern point of view. Nor did he think of these books as primarily historical.

The Pentateuch he thought of primarily as Law, setting forth the divine will for the regulation of life, and especially for the regulation of the cultus. That Law is represented as communicated in all its fullness and detail to Israel at the time of the Exodus, and while it is probable, as has been said above, that much of it reached its present form in a later age, there is no reason to doubt that the core of Israel's religious law dates from the time of Moses, and that it has been expanded and its principles re-applied to changing conditions in different ages. The early traditions of the book of Genesis, and the historical material in the other books of the Pentateuch, are not just aimlessly added, however.

To the Hebrew the will of God became known through concrete experience. His Law was not the fruit of his own speculation, but something given by a personal God through persons in living experience. Therefore the compiler of the Pentateuch is careful to record the story that provides the setting for the giving of the Law. So far as the main facts of the deliverance from Egypt under the leadership of Moses, and the establishment of the covenant of Sinai and the core of the sacred law are concerned, there is no reason to doubt that we are dealing with sound history. Beyond this, it is probable that much else that is reliably historical has been included. Yet it is impossible to treat the whole as strictly accurate, scientific history. But what the author is doing is expressing his profound conviction that the law was mediated in history. He offers the most circumstantial account of the history, not so much to draw attention to the detail itself, as through it to express his faith in that to which it testifies.

The whole story of the Exodus and the Covenant implies a doctrine of election, resting on the divine grace, and the writers, at every stage of the compilation of the Pentateuch, firmly believed in the election of Israel. Hence we have the recording of the traditions of the book of Genesis. If Israel was delivered from Egypt, how came she to be there? The E document was content to carry the story back to Abraham, while the J document went back to the beginnings of time. They are concerned to show the guiding hand of God in history, and to say that His interest in human history did not begin with the Exodus. Already before that His election of the patriarchs had taken place, and even from the first creation of man He had been concerned in man's affairs. Similarly the genealogies of the Priestly Code show an ever-narrowing line, as the divine election becomes more closely bound to the Israelite tribes. None of it is history for its own sake, but history that is related to the election and the covenant.

In the same way, when we come to the "historical books," we find again a religious interest predominant. A modern historian is concerned first to find the facts of history, and to collect and sift as fully as he can all the relevant facts of the situations he studies. But beyond that, he wishes to follow the trends and movements of history, to see, not a succession of moments of history, but a process, and to relate the course of history to the ideas and culture of those whose history it is. The Hebrew writer was more concerned to penetrate the significance of history, and to unfold to his fellows and those who should come after him the meaning for them of the things he recorded. And for him the significance was always a religious significance.

Hence the books of Joshua, Judges, Samuel and Kings are regarded by the Jews as prophetic books. They proclaim fundamental principles as unmistakably as the prophets in their oracles. The writer did not concern himself with recording all the facts, even all the facts which were most probably accessible to him. He singles out the facts that were relevant to his purpose. That there were lacunae in his story did not worry him. He wished rather to make each unit of his story inculcate the lesson that in loyalty and obedience to God was the way of wisdom for man. Within these books there is much excellent historical material, and the modern scientific historian will not withhold his admiration when he compares it with other ancient literature of comparable age, and when he thinks himself into the position of the writer and the research conditions of his time. But it was not facts for their own sake that the writer was seeking. He was rather through the facts exhorting men.

The remaining books that we think of as historical stand in the third division of the Hebrew canon. Chronicles, Ezra and Nehemiah form a continuous work covering in part the same ground as the books of Samuel and Kings. Here the writer supplements the facts he finds in the earlier works, but he also does not hesitate to alter what he finds before him. This is not because superior research facilities have enabled him to demonstrate that the earlier writer was inaccurate, but because in his view the facts were no longer edifying. Just as the Law had been re-adapted to changing conditions, so he was prepared to re-cast the facts of history to make them accord with the changed law of his day, so that it might teach godly lessons to his generation. More important to him than the facts was the meaning of the facts, and hence the facts could be sacrificed to the meaning.

It is probable that the reason why the Chronicler's work was not incorporated in the same division of the Canon as the earlier "historical works" was that that group of books had already acquired such a place in men's esteem that no other works of the same kind could hope to secure a place beside them. But beyond that, the books of Chronicles, Ezra and Nehemiah are not prophetic books, and could not properly be included in a prophetic canon. For while they seek to inculcate godly lessons, their primary interest is in the priestly law rather than in the prophetic principles. The author venerated all the priestly law of the Pentateuch, and the rules that governed the cultic usage of the Temple, and it was chiefly where he felt that the looser customs of an earlier age might undermine respect for the things he so much valued that he felt himself at liberty to change what he found in his sources.

The book of Esther is once more not so much history as propaganda, though this time less for prophetic principles or priestly laws, than for the spirit of Jewish nationalism. How far the writer was working with materials that possessed any historical value at all will be discussed below, but again he was less concerned with the truth of his facts than with the importance of the message he was delivering.

Any author is to be judged partly by the skill and success with which he carries through his purpose, and partly by the worth of the purpose he sets before him. The modern writer may pass a judgment on the value of the purpose the Hebrew writer entertained or the literary skill and resource he brought to his task. But he ought not to judge him by a purpose which was not his. The modern Old Testament historian will seek to sift the story, to see how far he can find historical material contained in it. But its worth as religious literature is quite other than that, and it was for this that it came into being. Whether it sets forth accurate history or not was of no more moment to its first readers than it is to many of its modern readers, who read it for edification rather than for education.

CHAPTER IV

THE BOOK OF JOSHUA

THE book of Joshua recounts the story of the conquest of Canaan by the united Israelite tribes under the leadership of Joshua, and of the subsequent apportionment of the land amongst the tribes. Jewish tradition, as recorded in the Talmud, attributes the book to the hand of Joshua, but this is to-day rejected no less decisively than the Mosaic authorship of the Pentateuch. The reasons for this include the following:

(a) the book includes an account of the death of Joshua and of subsequent events (xxiv. 29–33);

(b) it cites the book of Jashar (x. 13), which contained David's Lament on Saul and Jonathan, and which could not therefore have been compiled before the days of the monarchy;

(c) in a number of passages the age of the Conquest is looked back upon, apparently over a long interval (iv. 9, v. 9, vii. 26, viii. 28 f., ix. 27, x. 27, xiii. 13, xv. 63, xvi. 10);

(d) it relates the conquest of Leshem (= Laish) by the tribe of Dan (xix. 47), whereas Judges xviii states that much later than the time of the Conquest, when the tribe of Dan failed to maintain itself in its first location, it migrated to Laish and conquered it, taking the grandson of Moses as its priest;

(e) the dominant view of the book is that the Conquest was quickly achieved under the leadership of Joshua, and the whole land was conquered and almost all its inhabitants exterminated, whereas there are a number of fragments incorporated in the book presenting a different view (xiii. 13, xv. 13–19, 63, xvi. 10, xvii. 11–13, 16–18), and there is every reason to suppose that this latter view, which stands also in Judges i, is the more historical.

Apart from the inner inconsistency already noted, there are several others, giving the impression here, as in the Pentateuch, that a variety of sources have been drawn on. We find also some duplications comparable with the doublets in the Pentateuch. The following cases may be noted:

(*a*) according to iv. 9, Joshua set up twelve stones in the midst of the Jordan, while according to iv. 8, 20, the people carried twelve stones from the Jordan to Gilgal, where they were set up;

(*b*) in iii. 17 the people cross the Jordan, and in iv. 11 they again cross in the same direction;

(*c*) two different accounts of the fall of Jericho are interwoven in a single narrative, to the confusion of the reader, since according to the one account the people marched round the city seven times in silence, until, at the word of command, on the seventh circuit, they raised a loud shout, blew their trumpets and attacked the city, while according to the other account the sevenfold circuit of the city was headed by the priests blowing trumpets, and on the seventh circuit the walls collapsed, while in one place the sevenfold circuit would appear to occupy seven days, and in another to be achieved in a single day;

(*d*) we are told that in the battle for Ai Joshua set 30,000 men in ambush on the eve of the battle (viii. 3), and then later sent 5,000 men to the same spot for the same purpose (viii. 12);

(*e*) the king of Hebron is put to death in x. 26, and in x. 37 he again suffers the same fate;

(*f*) in chap. x, Hebron is taken by Joshua, and its inhabitants exterminated, while in xiv. 12 it is still uncaptured, and in xv. 14 it is captured by Caleb;

(*g*) in chaps. xxiii and xxiv we have two farewell addresses by Joshua.

It would therefore appear that here, as in the Pentateuch, we have a compilation from various sources, and it is generally believed that they are continuations of the sources drawn on for the Pentateuch. Material from J, E, D, and P stands here, and Eissfeldt finds material from his source L embodied in chaps. ii–vii and xxiv. It is not to be supposed, however, that the Pentateuch and Joshua ever formed a single work. It is the sources that overlap into this book, not the compilation. Indeed, the whole process of editing is different from that of the Pentateuch. There the book of Deuteronomy stood apart, while the framework of the rest of the Pentateuch was provided by P; here the framework is provided by D, and material from J and E, probably already combined in a single account, was incorporated, while the P material appears to have been added later. It will be seen below that all of the Former Prophets show the marks of the Deuteronomic school in their editing, and the book of Joshua is therefore at one with the rest of the books in this collection, so far as its first edition is concerned. It differs from the other books, however, in the amount of the P material which has been added. This material stands almost wholly in the second half of the book, and is concerned with the statistical and geographical matter which is there found. In the remaining books of the Former Prophets there is practically no material from the hand of P, or presupposing a knowledge of P.

It should be added that the ascription of material to P does not imply that it is worthless, and especially is this true of the geographical material found in this book. Alt finds evidence of the use of a pre-monarchical document in chaps. xiii–xix, save that chap. xv is held to rest on a document of the time of Josiah, while Albright would put this latter document yet earlier.

In its first form the book of Joshua could not have been earlier than the promulgation of D, while in its present form it could not be earlier than the issue of P. We are therefore carried down to the fourth century B.C. for the finished work. But here, as in the Pentateuch, the sources are recognized to be very much older. The JE traditions incorporated must be carried back much farther, while in the poetic citation in x. 12 f. we are carried back still farther. The book of Jashar from which it is taken, cannot be older than the time of David, and it is possible that it contained a later poem, and comes from a time not earlier than the period of Solomon (see page 75). But the poems of the book of Jashar were older than the collection, and this one may well have been contemporary with the events it commemorates.

By some the word Jashar is connected with Jeshurun, a poetic name for Israel, and the book is believed to have been a collection of national songs. By others the name is read as the first word of the opening poem, in accordance with the practice whereby the Hebrew names for the books of the Pentateuch

consist of either the initial words, or words found near the beginning. Be that as it may, the poem here cited is doubtless ancient,
and a fragment of a national poem, celebrating a victory of
Joshua's, and giving to this particular exploit of his an earlier
attestation than any other, and so connecting his work securely
with the Central Highlands.

The setting of the quotation tells how Joshua made a forced
march in the night to come to the aid of the hard-pressed
Gibeonites, and how his attack coincided with a portentous
storm, which threw the enemy into confusion. The comment on
the citation says that the day was preter-naturally lengthened,
and the sun remained in the sky far beyond its appointed time.
This is not relevant to the situation, for sunshine would hardly
mark so violent a storm. Moreover, the poem depicts the sun
as over Gibeon and the moon as over Aijalon, with the speaker,
presumably, between them. These would appear to be morning
conditions, at the time of dawn. Further, the Hebrew says
"Sun, be silent," i.e., do not shine. The cry is therefore for the
prolongation of darkness, to enable the Israelites to reach their
foes under cover of night, at the close of their forced march, and
it would seem to have been answered by the brewing storm, and
then by its breaking. To represent this poetically as the sun and
moon standing still is skilful and effective, just as the Song of
Deborah acknowledges the help of the elements in the defeat of
Sisera by saying "The stars in their courses fought against
Sisera" (Judges v. 20).

It is believed that this quotation stood originally in J. Since
J and E cannot be separated in Joshua with any security, and
since this poem deals with a victory of the Ephraimite Joshua in
the central part of the land, it might be supposed that it would
more naturally stand in E. It has to be remembered, however,
that the book of Jashar contained a poem of David's, and
possibly some Solomonic material. It was probably a southern
collection, therefore, made perhaps during the period of the
united monarchy, and it could thus be quite naturally cited in
the southern corpus of national traditions.

CHAPTER V

THE BOOK OF JUDGES

THE book of Judges ostensibly recounts the history of Israel from the death of Joshua to the eve of the founding of the monarchy. It presents us with a series of "Judges," who are not to be thought of forensically, but rather as national heroes and leaders, and deals primarily with their exploits. It does not attempt to give us any general history of the period, though it gives us some vivid insights into the conditions of the times.

The book falls into three distinct parts. These are:

(*a*) i. 1–ii. 5, in which we find brief notes on the partial conquest of the land of Canaan;

(*b*) ii. 6–xvi. 31, in which the traditions of some of the judges, and the mere names of others, are recorded, together with the story of Abimelech;

(*c*) xvii–xxi, in which two stories, unrelated to any of the Judges, are narrated.

The first of these sections stands in marked contrast to the book of Joshua. There the conquest of the land is represented as the achievement of a united Israel under the leadership of Joshua, whereas here it is represented as the work of the separate tribes, each fighting for its own hand, though sometimes in local combinations, after the death of Joshua. Moreover, several of the verses of this chapter stand in almost identical form in the book of Joshua, and provide those traces of a variant tradition, to which reference has been made above.

According to the book of Joshua, the division of the land was made after the Conquest, whereas according to this, it was made before the Conquest. It has been observed above that the conquest of Laish, which was really effected by the tribe of Dan after the time of Joshua, is ante-dated in the time of that leader by the book of Joshua. It now appears from these fragments, which are believed to belong to the J cycle, that the dominant impression of the book of Joshua is unhistorical. The work of Joshua lay in the central part of the land, though it is clear that even here the conquest was by no means complete, and that many of the towns that were ultimately incorporated in the tribes of Ephraim and Manasseh were unconquered in his time, or for some considerable time afterwards.

The second section of the book of Judges is its main part, and it employs a schematic framework, into which the stories of the individual Judges are placed. This is very similar to what we shall find later in the books of Kings, after the time of the disruption, and here, as there, the point of view of the author of the framework is characteristic of Deuteronomy. But whereas in the books of Kings it is determined by the Deuteronomic law of the single sanctuary, here it rests on the Deuteronomic principle that national fortunes and religious loyalty go hand in hand. For since the single legitimate sanctuary recognized by the Deuteronomic school had not yet been built, it was out of the question here to employ the principle that served for the books of Kings.

The philosophy of history that dominates all the story is that religious declension brings national weakness and foreign oppression, until God in His grace raises up a leader who both recalls the people to loyalty and delivers them from their oppressors, giving them a peace that lasts through all his days and beyond, to be followed then by fresh defection and disaster. Twelve Judges are named, but six of them are mere names— viz., Shamgar (iii. 31), Tola (x. 1 f.), Jair (x. 3–5), Ibzan (xii. 8– 10), Elon (xii. 11 f.), and Abdon (xii. 13–15)—while of the other six exploits are related—viz., Othniel, Ehud, Deborah, Gideon, Jephthah and Samson. All are integrated into a careful chronological scheme, but if the figures for the periods of the various Judges and for the times of rest are added together, an impossibly high total is reached. For 1 Kings vi. 1 estimates the period from the Exodus to the founding of the Temple at 480 years. If we deduct from this the period of the Wandering in the Wilderness and the period of Joshua, together with the period of Samuel, Saul and David, we are left with far less than the book of Judges requires.

The predominance of the round figures of twenty years, forty years and eighty years in the chronology is an indication that it is an artificial one, reckoning in terms of half generations, generations, and two generations, and little reliance can be placed upon it. Yet it is thought by some scholars that both these figures and that of 1 Kings vi. 1 came from the same circles, and that they were not intended to be inconsistent with one another. Hence they hold that the years of foreign domination are not to be reckoned in addition to the periods of the Judges, but to be regarded as included in them, and that Abimelech and Saul, who were regarded by the Deuteronomic editors of the historical books as usurpers, were not separately reckoned in estimating the total. An alternative view is that of Garstang, who thinks the Minor Judges and Abimelech are to be disregarded. It is more probable that the figure of 1 Kings vi. 1 is a round one, reached not by elaborate manipulation of the figures given in the book of Judges, but by reckoning forty years each to the twelve great national leaders from Moses to Solomon, counting the six major Judges, Moses, Joshua, Eli, Samuel, Saul and David.

It is probable that the Judges were local, rather than national, heroes and deliverers, and their periods may have been very close to one another, or even have overlapped. But when once we have recognized the chronology to be artificial, we are left with no materials for the chronology of the period. The date of the Exodus is placed by some in the fifteenth century B.C., and by others in the thirteenth century B.C., and while the former would allow the 480 years of 1 Kings vi. 1 to the founding of the Temple, the other would seem to curtail the period of the Judges too much. It should be remembered, however, that many scholars believe that not all the Israelite tribes went down to Egypt, and that some entered the land of Canaan in the fourteenth century and others in the thirteenth. Since the book of Judges recounts exploits of leaders of both groups of tribes in the post-Settlement period, some may have taken place in the time before the later group of immigrants entered the land. The curtailment of the period is less serious than might be supposed, therefore. Indeed, the earlier group of immigrants, on this view, entered the land in precisely the age when the whole of the tribes entered, on the view that all the tribes came out of Egypt in the fifteenth century B.C. The total period of the Judges is therefore precisely the same on both of these views.

The stories which the compiler placed in his framework were taken from older sources, and once more we find that some of them appear to be composite, showing that we are again working with materials drawn from two corpora of traditions. These are commonly referred to by the symbols J and E, though it is by no means to be inferred that these stories once stood in continuous documents with J and E. What is meant is rather that the circles from which J and E emanated also collected cycles of the traditions of the post-settlement period and that those cycles have been drawn on by the compiler of our book. It is, indeed, more probable that the sources of the book of Judges are continuous with some of the sources of the books of Samuel than with those of the earlier books. In both two main collections appear to have been drawn on, though the books of Samuel seem to have drawn on a larger number of subsidiary sources. It should be added that Eissfeldt has again found traces of a third cycle in the book of Judges, which he would connect with his L source of the Pentateuch.

The indications of at least two sources are particularly strong in the case of the story of Gideon. Here even the casual reader will observe with some surprise that after the Midianites have been scattered and their chiefs slain (vii. 24–viii. 3), they still have to be pursued and fresh chiefs have to be slain (viii. 4–21), while the following verses (viii. 22–27) appear to resume the former of these accounts. Similarly the Abimelech story and the Jephthah story are resolved into two. In the case of the story of Deborah we have a prose account, side by side with an ancient poetic account, and combined with the prose account we have the story of a completely separate incident. In Judges iv. we read that Jabin, king of Hazor, is the oppressor of Israel, and Sisera, who dwelt in Harosheth, is his commander-in-chief. The victory is won by members of the tribes of Zebulun and Naphtali only.

In the poetic account of Judges v, Sisera is no mere servant, but the head of the enemy coalition, whose mother is waited on by princesses, while the victory is achieved by members of a number of the Israelite tribes, from both north and south of the Vale of Esdraelon. Here there is no mention of Jabin whatever. It is therefore probable that in chap. iv a quite separate story of the victory of the two tribes of Zebulun and Naphtali over the neighbouring Canaanite king of Hazor has been combined with the victory of Deborah and Barak over Sisera. In Joshua xi the victory over Jabin king of Hazor is attributed to Joshua, and since it is more probable that the great name of Joshua would attract to itself the victory of these northern tribes than that they should be given the glory of a victory which was really won by Joshua, historical value may be given to the Jabin elements of the story of Judges iv, when its literary separation from the Sisera story is recognized.

For the victory over Sisera, the Song of Deborah is of primary importance. Here we have again an old national song, probably contemporary with the events it describes, and coming from the twelfth century B.C. It is thus one ot the oldest monuments of Hebrew literature that we possess, and while parts of the Blessing of Jacob may be older, and some of the smaller poetic pieces which have been noticed above, we have nothing of comparable length which is so old. Its fine vigour and its superb literary quality are especially noteworthy in view of its great antiquity. Here, as in the case of the Joshua poem, we find the prose narrator presents a story in some respects discrepant with the poetry. In the prose account of Judges iv, Sisera meets his end at the hand of Jael when he is asleep, after having been lured by her false promises to put himself so help-lessly into her power. But according to the poetic account, he is felled to the ground by Jael when he is on the point of drinking the curdled milk she has brought at his request. For a woman to attack an armed warrior from before, even though she chooses her moment of vantage, is an act of great courage and resource, and far removed from the low treachery of the prose account. Here there was no invitation to Sisera to accept the hospitality of her tent, nor was he allowed to taste the drink he had solicited, but with swift action she seized a mallet and dealt him the fatal blow in the moment when he bent his head to drink.

The third section of the book of Judges consists of the story of Micah's image and its removal to Dan, when Danites migrated to Laish and conquered it, taking with them Micah's image and his priest, together with the story of the outrage at Gibeah and the subsequent war between the other Israelite tribes and Benjamin, leading to the rape of the maidens of Shiloh. These stories stand completely outside the chronological scheme of the book, and both appear to be composite. They therefore seem to have stood in the two source books which the compiler of the book of Judges used, though at what point in those books they stood we have no means of knowing. It may well be that the compiler is responsible for their relegation to the appendix, since they have no direct relation to any of the Judges, and therefore could not be integrated into the main part of his book. The Deuteronomic hostility to the sanctuary at Dan, which comes out in the framework to the books of Kings, may have dictated the preservation of this story of the origin of the sanctuary in idolatry and theft. The other story probably once stood in close connexion with the story of Saul. It tells how the people of Jabesh Gilead gave their daughters in marriage to the Benjamites, and so explains why they appealed for help to Gibeah when they were in trouble, and found a response under the leadership of Saul (1 Sam. xi). If the suggestion recorded above is correct, that to the Deuteronomic school Saul was a usurper whose years like those of oppressors, were merely subsumed under the periods of the legitimate leaders, it may have been that the opportunity to record the infamy of Saul's tribe could not be missed.

Many of the stories of the book of Judges, and especially the two that close the book, form somewhat unsavoury reading. Their historical value, is, however, beyond question, and the insight into the social, moral and religious conditions of the period following the settlement which they give is of the highest importance. For here again, while the book of Judges cannot have been compiled before the promulgation of the Code of Deuteronomy, whose influence it so largely shows, its material is of much greater antiquity. The cycles of traditions on which it draws were much older, and the traditions themselves were doubtless older than the collections in which they stood. Auerbach has argued that in Judges i we have extracts that go back to a document much older than J, by whose school it may have been preserved for us, and that it stands very close to the events it records, while it is highly probable that the Song of Deborah is even closer to the events of which it sings.

CHAPTER VI

THE BOOKS OF SAMUEL

THE books of Samuel form a single book in Hebrew MSS., though printed editions of the Hebrew Bible follow the division into two, which was first made in the Greek version. The whole should quite certainly be treated, therefore, as a single continuous work. Whether we should go farther and regard the books of Kings as also a part of the same work is another matter. The Greek Bible calls Samuel and Kings the four books of Kingdoms.

The books of Samuel narrate the story of the birth and childhood of Samuel, of the capture and return of the Ark, of the Philistine control and the establishment of the monarchy, and then of the reigns of Saul and David. According to the Talmud Samuel was the author of the book, but this is manifestly wrong, since Samuel dies before the story has more than half run its course. A number of modern scholars believe that the story of the birth of Samuel was originally the story of the birth of Saul, and that it has been transferred to Samuel. This is because the word-play in 1 Sam. i. 20 would be more obviously relevant to the name of Saul.[1] But plays on proper names even more far-fetched than this are found elsewhere in the Old Testament. Moreover the birth story would seem to lead to the dedication of the child to the service of the Shiloh sanctuary, where the Ark was. The connexion of the Ark with the tribe of Ephraim is well established, but we have no information which would render probable the bringing of a Benjamite into association with it.

That the work rests on a variety of sources becomes clear on the most superficial reading. In 1 Sam. vii. 13 we read that after the deliverance of Mizpah the Philistines came no more

---

[1] "Because I have asked him (*sh⁰'iltîw*) of the Lord." This is nearer to *Shā'ul* (= Saul) than to *Sh⁰mū'ēl* (= Samuel).

within the borders of Israel all the days of Samuel, and in the following chapter the desire of the people for a king is ascribed to no higher motive than their eagerness to imitate the heathen nations around them. But in ix. 16 we read that the establishment of the monarchy was by divine initiative, and was effected through the same Samuel in order to save Israel out of the hand of the Philistines. In x. 24 Saul is proclaimed king, but in the following chapter he is engaged on the farm, and when messengers from Jabesh Gilead come seeking help, they do not apply to him. It is only when he finds by casual inquiry what the trouble is that he assumes the lead, and as the result of his energetic action he is elected king.

As perplexing is the story of David's introduction to the court of Saul. In 1 Sam. xvi he is brought as a stranger to the court of Saul in order to soothe him with music when his disorder comes upon him. Thereupon he becomes Saul's armour-bearer, for he is already a man of war. Yet in the following chapter, when Israel was at war with the Philistines, David was not with the king, as we should expect, but at home on the farm, and when he came to the camp it was to bring food to his brothers, and to incur their rebuke for coming out of idle curiosity to watch the battle. Clearly David was now a mere lad. Yet when he returns from killing Goliath, the king, who had no idea who he was, took him home and suffered him no more to return to his father. Manifestly there are two accounts of the foundation of the monarchy and two of David's introduction to the court of Saul.

So far as the setting up of the monarchy is concerned, these accounts were marked by a complete difference of attitude to that institution. To the writer of the one, the monarchy was God's way of bringing deliverance to His people, while to the other the establishment of the kingdom was an act of rebellion against God, and of rejection of His rule. When once we have distinguished these two sources, we find that there are some duplicate accounts of similar incidents, which, though not directly contradictory, may with probability be distributed between our two sources. Thus there are two accounts of David's flight to Achish (xxi. 10–15; xxvii. 5–12), two accounts of David's sparing Saul's life (xxiv. 1–22; xxvi. 1–25), and perhaps two of the death of Saul (1 Sam. xxxi. 1–7; 2 Sam. i. 1–16).

Some writers have analysed the whole work on a two source theory, assigning almost everything to one or other of the two sources above distinguished. They then connect these sources with the J and E sources of the Pentateuch. It is much more likely, however, that we should connect them with the sources of the book of Judges, and it has already been said that we cannot prove that the sources of the book of Judges have any documentary unity with the sources of the Pentateuch. Rost argues, indeed, that the two main sources of the books of Samuel cannot be connected with any source drawn on for any other book, with the exception of 1 Kings i f. To the present writer it seems probable that there was documentary unity between the sources of Judges and Samuel. But this no more establishes community of authorship for the two works than documentary unity of the sources of the Pentateuch and Joshua establishes community of origin of these books. It should be added that Eissfeldt once more finds his third source connected with L.

These schemes seem unduly simple, however. On the two source view the infancy stories of Samuel connect with the E cycle, while in 2 Sam. there is a long continuous narrative which is ascribed to J (ix–xx). This is longer than any continuous extract from a single document found in any of the books so far studied, with the exception of Deuteronomy. A few Deuteronomic additions are found in the work, but on this view it may be regarded as a work which was compiled before the Deuteronomic reform, to which a few touches were subsequently added, just as Joshua is regarded as a fundamentally Deuteronomic work to which P material was subsequently added. The books of Samuel would then be the only fundamentally pre-Deuteronomic work included in the canon of the Former Prophets.

A more complex view of the origin of our work is taken by Kennedy, and one which seems to do more justice to the facts. He finds a number of separate sources, and instead of assigning the later history of the establishment of the monarchy and its associated narratives to the circles from which E emanated, he assigns it to Deuteronomic circles. This brings the work closer

THE FORMER PROPHETS 67

into line with the other books of this division of the Canon. The sources he distinguishes are:

(a) one dealing with the infancy of Samuel;

(b) one dealing with the history of the Ark;

(c) a history of the monarchy, favourable to the institution;

(d) a Deuteronomic history of the monarchy unfavourable to it;

(e) a Court History of David, from which 2 Sam. ix-xx was taken.

The compilation of the present book he then places later than the preparation of the Deuteronomic history, and hence towards the end of the Exile. This would seem to be unduly late. For it is probable that the books of Samuel were completed before the books of Kings were compiled, whether the two originally formed a single work or not, and there is no reason to suppose that the compilation of the books of Kings was so late as the end of the exile. Hence, while we may with probability recognize the use of a variety of sources, we need not ascribe the later history of the establishment of the monarchy to post-Deuteronomic days. For if, as many scholars believe, Hos. x. 9 is a condemnation of the setting up of the kingdom, the point of view of this document can be found in an eighth century prophet. We are then free to ascribe the compilation of this book to the Deuteronomic circles that appear to have prepared a series of works covering the history from the Settlement to the Exile.

As in the previous works examined above, the recognition of the late character of the work does not detract from its historical worth, when the earliness of the sources employed is remembered. At the same time it should never be forgotten that the writers were not interested in scientific history, in the modern sense. They were interested in the lessons of history, and even more in religion, whose ends their narration was intended to serve. Nevertheless, the earlier sources are of particularly high value for the unvarnished simplicity with which they tell their story, and the vividness of their narration. Here what Kennedy calls the Court History of David calls for especial mention. This makes no attempt to conceal the faults of David or to gloss over the troubles which he had to face. There is no reason whatever to doubt that this is of very early date, not far removed from the time of David himself, and there is no historical writing of comparable length in any known literature of the world that can stand beside it in age, lucidity and honesty.

Something should again be said of ancient poems which are preserved in the books of Samuel. Here we find:

(*a*) The Song of Hannah (1 Sam. ii. 1–10). This was quite clearly not composed by Hannah. The line "the barren hath borne seven" can claim some appropriateness to the occasion, though no very strict accord with Hannah's experience. But the couplet "He shall give strength unto his king, and exalt the horn of his anointed" could not have been written in pre-monarchic days. When once it is recognized that the Song is not Hannah's, its precise age must be left undetermined. It may have been a psalm for the community, commemorating the saving mercies of God.

(*b*) David's Lament over Saul and Jonathan (2 Sam. i. 19–27). This is extracted from the book of Jashar, to which reference has already been made, and its genuineness as a Davidic poem is generally agreed. The absence of any reference to the strained relations between Saul and David is in favour of its genuineness. Such magnanimity is remarkable enough in David, but it would be more surprising if it were attributed to him without basis by another, who would much more naturally have made some reference to Saul's hostility. Moreover, the poem has no religious allusion. In view of the strong tradition which associated the name of David with religious poetry, another writer would probably have taken care to give a religious character to his poem. The only positive indication of Davidic authorship in the poem is its reference to the close affection between Jonathan and the poet (i. 26).

(*c*) David's Lament over Abner (2 Sam. iii. 33 f.). This brief lament may also with probability be ascribed to David. The resource with which David attended in person as the chief mourner at Abner's funeral carries its own conviction. For Joab could not be punished for exercising his legal right of blood revenge, yet if nothing were done David could hardly escape the suspicion of complicity in the deed which removed Abner from his way. But by appearing at the funeral in this role, the king was able to dissociate himself from the act with great effectiveness. And since there is every reason to believe that David had poetic gifts, there is no reason to doubt that he composed an appropriate elegy, of which a fragment has survived.

(d) The Hymn of David (2 Sam. xxii = Ps. xviii). This stands in the appendix to the book, to which reference will be made below. It was probably not inserted there until long after the compilation of the book. When it was inserted, it was doubtless already old, and believed to be by David. But the interval since his time was now so great that there can be no certainty of its authorship, though many scholars concede that it may be David's. They find a number of later elements and glosses in it, however, and Kennedy thinks the whole poem can therefore with more appropriateness be regarded as later.

(e) The Testament of David (2 Sam. xxiii. 1–7). This also stands in the appendix, where it was a late addition. In its opening couplet it purports to be the work of David. There are few who allow the claim, since it is doubted whether David would have referred to himself as "the beloved of the songs of Israel." Yet though the poem was not brought into the book of Samuel until a post-exilic date, it was probably an ancient composition.

Something must be said about the appendix to these books. Here, as in the case of Judges, we have some items appended, without chronological integration into the story. But here there is no reason to suppose that the compiler of the book was responsible for this addition, in its present form. For the Appendix bears the marks of a history of its own. It consists of six sections: (a) the Famine and its removal (2 Sam. xxi. 1–14), (b) Exploits of David's warriors (xxi. 15–22), (c) David's Hymn (xxii), (d) David's Testament (xxiii. 1–7), (e) David's Mighty Men and their exploits (xxiii. 8–39), (f) the Census and the Plague (xxiv). It will be seen that the first and last of these are of similar character, the second and the fifth belong together, while the third and fourth are both poems ascribed to David. Apparently (a) and (f) once stood together in the Appendix, but were separated by the insertion of (b) and (e), which were then continuous, until (c) and (d) were inserted into their midst.

We are therefore carried down to a late date before the Appendix reached its present form. Its materials, however, are of undeniable antiquity, and Elliger has argued that xxiii. 24–39 may date from David's Hebron rule. It is possible that the first form of the Appendix, containing (a) and (f), was added by the first compiler of the book. The stories of the Famine and the Plague might well be thought worthy of preservation, just as the stories in the appendix to the book of Judges were, and the Deuteronomic editor might well be glad to record the nemesis that befell the house of Saul, since he probably shared the anti-Benjamite feeling that inspired the compiler of the book of Judges, while he would have an interest in recording the event that gave sanctity to the site of David's altar, which became the site of the Temple which was so dear to the whole Deuteronomic school.

Since the Chronicler ignores all that stands in what has been called the Court History of David (2 Sam. ix–xx), some editors believe that these chapters were at one time excised from the work and subsequently restored. It seems improbable that they would have been added to the work so late as after the time of the Chronicler, and since a sufficient reason for the Chronicler's non-use of their material can be found without resort to this hypothesis, it seems wiser to reject it. To the Chronicler it would not appear conducive to good morals, or appropriate to the glory of the by now idealized king, to record his sins and his misfortunes. For the same reasons it is very improbable that after the time of the Chronicler anyone would have taken the veil from these things to insert them in a work where they were not already found.

CHAPTER VII

THE BOOKS OF KINGS

THE Books of Kings again form a single book in Hebrew MSS., and the division into two was first made by the Septuagint, whence it was copied into the Latin Bible and into modern versions. As has been said, the Greek Bible regards it as the continuation of the books of Samuel in a single work. In favour of this view, which is shared by some modern writers, is the fact that the opening section of 1 Kings is quite certainly the continuation of the document which provided 2 Sam. ix–xx. If the appendix to 2 Sam. is ignored, therefore, these passages are brought into immediate connexion. Against the view that Samuel and Kings formed a single work is the consideration that the method of compilation is more stereotyped in the books of Kings than in the books of Samuel. Yet even here it should be remembered that the stereotyped formulae begin only with the Disruption. Moreover, even if we have a separate work, the two books must have followed one another within a very few years, and the one must have been written expressly to continue the other.

The work opens with the story of the succession troubles that marked the end of David's life, and then deals with the reign of Solomon at some length, but far less fully than the previous work has dealt with the life of David. The central point of the account of Solomon's reign is the erection of the Temple. Then follows an account of the Disruption, and of the history of the divided kingdom. It is here that the framework appears. Throughout the period from the Disruption to the end of the northern kingdom, we have a parallel history, which may be compared to a person walking, who advances first one foot and then the other. The story of one kingdom is carried forward, and then the writer turns to the other kingdom and continues its story until it is ahead. For each reign there is an opening formula and a closing formula, and the opening formula for the kings of Judah is fuller than that for the kings of Israel. For the kings of Israel the opening formula gives (*a*) the synchronism of the accession with the regnal year of the sister kingdom, (*b*) the length of the reign, and (*c*) the writer's judgment on the reign. For the kings of Judah, we find, in addition to these three items (*d*) the age of the king at his accession, and (*e*) his mother's name. In the closing formula we find (*a*) a reference to the sources where the interested reader may find further information, (*b*) a notice of the king's death and burial, and (*c*) his successor's name.

The judgments on the kings all reflect the standpoint of a Deuteronomic editor. The Israelite kings are condemned without exception, and usually compared with Jeroboam, whose oft-recalled offence was the creation of rival shrines to the Jerusalem Temple. In all the judgments on the kings of Judah the question of the centralization of the cult figures. This is seen particularly in the case of the good kings, where the favourable judgment is sometimes tempered with the observation that nevertheless they did not remove the high places (1 Kings xv. 14, xxii. 43). The same religious pragmatism that we have found in the framework of the book of Judges is found here, in the effort to relate the fortunes of the kings to their religious attitude. Further, in the account of the reign of Solomon, not alone is the central interest in the creation of the Temple, which was of so great importance in Deuteronomic eyes, but the material is so arranged as to point to a connexion between Solomon's love of foreign wives and toleration of foreign cults, and the misfortunes suffered by the king and the state. There are also in the work innumerable marks of the influence of the style of Deuteronomy.

It is therefore certain that the book was compiled by an editor who belonged to the Deuteronomic school. It carries the story down to the year 561 B.C., when Jehoiachin was released from prison on the accession of Evil-merodach. There is certainly no reason to come down much below this date for the writing of the book, since it is difficult to believe that if the editor had lived to see the fall of Babylon and the Persian permission for the exiles to return he would have refrained from mentioning it. It is probable, indeed, that we should go back earlier than this date for the composition of the book, and find in the verses about Jehoiachin's release a subsequent addition. Some scholars go much farther than this, and believe that the work originally stopped with the reign of Jehoiachin, and the first deportation of Nebuchadrezzar in 597 B.C. There are, indeed, some touches in the work that would seem to imply that it was written before the end of the rule of the Davidic dynasty in Jerusalem, and the destruction of the Temple (cf. 1 Kings viii. 8, xi. 36, 2 Kings viii. 19), and this would seem to confirm the view that the work as a whole was compiled before the fall of Jerusalem in 586 B.C. The chapters dealing with the siege and destruction of Jerusalem, and with the governorship of Gedaliah, may well have been added by the same hand within a few years of the first composition of the book.

Once more we must distinguish between the age of the work and the age of the material it incorporates. The writer frequently refers the reader to other works where he may find fuller information, and these have doubtless been drawn on for the compilation. Other works not specifically named seem also to have been drawn on. The sources used appear to have included at least the following:

(*a*) The Court History of David, which provided 2 Sam. ix–xx. This has supplied 1 Kings i. 1–ii. 11.

(*b*) The Acts of Solomon (1 Kings xi. 41). This was probably an early chronicle of the reign of Solomon, which may date from the ninth century B.C.

(*c*) A Royal History of Judah. This is referred to again and again, as the "Book of the Chronicles of the Kings of Judah." It is, of course, to be clearly distinguished from the canonical books of Chronicles.

(*d*) A Royal History of Israel. This is similarly referred to often, and is even more obviously to be distinguished from our books of Chronicles, since the latter ignore the northern kingdom, save where the southern kingdom was concerned in its history. Both of these sources (*c*) and (*d*) appear to have been of too informal a character to have been official court records, and they are best thought of as lost popular histories.

(*e*) A special source dealing with the period of Ahab, who

receives disproportionate treatment. Oesterley and Robinson think of this as an Acts of Ahab, while others think it was of rather wider interest, and offered a history of the Syrian Wars.

(*f*) A Temple History. If there was a history of the Ark, as postulated by Kennedy in treating of the books of Samuel, it would be easily credible that there should be a history of the Temple, which would be of special interest to our compiler.

(*g*) Prophetic Biographies. How many of these were used we cannot say, but in addition to the cycles of stories dealing with Elijah, Elisha and Isaiah, we find the story of Micaiah ben Imlah (1 Kings xxii). We should perhaps rather speak of the sagas of Elijah and Elisha, since they are far more embellished with wonder stories than the others, though we are not necessarily carried far below the period of Elijah and Elisha for their composition.

It will be seen, therefore, that there is every reason to believe that there was continuous literary activity in the field of history and biography in Israel, and books may have been written in much larger number than we can know between the Court History of David and the work of the Deuteronomic school. At the same time, it must never be forgotten that the authors of the canonical books, and probably of the sources on which they rest, were never interested primarily in the facts of history, but in the meaning of history, and particularly in the religious meaning it had. It is for this reason that Omri is dismissed with very slight reference (1 Kings xvi. 23–28), despite the fact that he must have been one of the ablest of the Israelite kings. We know from the Moabite Stone that it was Omri who conquered Moab, and that the revolt of which we read in 2 Kings i. 1 was made after forty years of subjection. We also know from Assyrian inscriptions that after his very dynasty had perished, his country was still known as the land of Omri. The high lights of the work are always reserved for the events of crucial religious importance—the founding of the Temple, the Disruption with the consequent elevation of Dan and Bethel to be royal shrines, the social and religious crisis in the time of Ahab, the reforms of Hezekiah and Josiah, and the deliverance of Jerusalem from Sennacherib's arms by divine intervention.

Of poetic fragments incorporated in the books of Kings,

THE FORMER PROPHETS 75

two only call for notice. The first is the Dedication Formula at
the dedication of the Temple (1 Kings viii. 13). This stands
somewhat differently in the Septuagint version, where a note is
added to the effect that the fragment stands in the Book of the
Song. The word "song" would be represented in Hebrew MSS.
by *shyr*, which may be a metathesis of *yshr*, which is how the
Book of *Jashar* would be represented. Hence it is possible that
this is an extract from the same Book of Jashar, of which we
have found other traces. If this is correct, the date of that
collection would be brought down to not earlier than the time
of Solomon, but there is no need to bring it down any later,
or to doubt that we have here a genuine fragment of a poem
which is as old as Solomon's time.

The other is the Psalm of Isaiah (2 Kings xix. 21–31). This
is found in one of the duplicated sections of the Bible. A good
deal of the books of Samuel and Kings was incorporated in the
books of Chronicles, as will be said below, but there are also
some passages which stand in 2 Kings and in Isaiah (2 Kings
xviii. 13–xx. 19 = Isa. xxxvi–xxxix, with some exceptions),
or in 2 Kings and in Jeremiah (2 Kings xxiv. 18–xxv. 30 = Jer.
lii, again with some exceptions). This Psalm of Isaiah is thus
found also in Isa. xxxvii. 22–32, with minor variations. As
2 Kings xix. 32 appears to have connected with verse 20, it
would appear that the poem was inserted into the context after
the compilation of the section. It should be added that it is
more probable that the editors of Isaiah and Jeremiah borrowed
these sections from the book of Kings than that the borrowing
was the other way round.

Reviewing the books of this division of the Hebrew Canon
of the Old Testament, we see that there is some reason to place
them all within a relatively short period, between 621 B.C. and
586 B.C. The Deuteronomic school of writers must therefore
have been very active in the period, and they seem to have
undertaken the preparation of a general history of Israel from
the Settlement to their own time. The first form of the book of
Joshua came from their hand and also the book of Judges,
including its appendix. It is possible that the books of Samuel
already existed, and were incorporated in their work, though it
seems more probable that these books were prepared in order

to continue the story from the point where the book of Judges
lays it down.

The books of Kings were almost certainly written to bring
the story down to their own time. It is quite improbable,
however, that a single hand was responsible for the editing of
all these books, since the editorial methods vary in the different
books. All that we can say with any confidence is that the whole
of the Former Prophets came from this school within a generation of the publication of Deuteronomy. With the possible
exception of the books of Samuel, all were first prepared, on
the basis of older sources, by the Deuteronomic school in
their present form, though the book of Joshua received some
substantial additions from the hand of the priestly school in a
later age, while only very minor additions were made to the
other books, including at least some parts of the appendix to
the books of Samuel.

BOOK III
THE LATTER PROPHETS

CHAPTER VIII

THE NATURE OF PROPHECY

WE come now to the books we commonly think of as the prophetic books, i.e., the books which contain the oracles of some of the prophets, together with incidents from their lives. Not all of the prophets figure here, while the book of Daniel, that we place among the prophets in our Bibles, following the Greek Bible, stands outside the prophetic collection in the Hebrew Bible. It may be that the reason was that the books of the prophetic Canon had already acquired too great a place in men's esteem for other books to have had any chance of coming in beside them, or it may be that it was felt to be a book of another kind.

It is more surprising that the oracles of no prophets earlier than the eighth century are found here. It has been said above that cycles of stories dealing with Elijah and Elisha were drawn on by the compiler of the books of Kings. We might have expected such cycles to have been preserved along with the canonical prophets, in view of the great place which Elijah and Elisha held in the tradition. It may be that they were no longer extant in the post-exilic age when these books were being gathered together.

The Old Testament prophets have been regarded as a unique feature of Israelite religious life, but modern study has tended to rob them of this glory. There are accounts in the Old Testament which portray prophets as behaving with strange abandon, to which the not very appropriate name of ecstasy has become attached. Sometimes they were influenced by music, and sometimes by group psychology, which made them throw off all restraint and do the most unusual things. Even the greater prophets, whose oracles stand in the prophetic canon, could sometimes do strange things, as when Isaiah went about in Jerusalem naked and barefoot (Isa. xx), or Jeremiah appeared with a wooden yoke round his neck (Jer. xxvii f.). Within the Old Testament there is a considerable amount of evidence of abnormal behaviour on the part of prophets, and some evidence that to the eye of the observer there was nothing to distinguish the prophet from the madman. Hence the prophet has been thought of in terms of the dervish, and evidence has been adduced that he was not unique in the ancient world. Amongst the surrounding peoples men of the same kind were found, and the Old Testament itself provides evidence in the account of Elijah's contest on Mt. Carmel that men of this kind were found in the service of Baal, and were called by the name of prophets.

These prophets were often gregarious in Israel, as were the Baal prophets on Mt. Carmel, and evidence has been collected to show that there were associations of such prophets attached to the cult throughout the world in which Israel lived. For the Old Testament contains much to suggest that the prophets were not, as a whole, hostile to the priesthood and the cultus, but that there were prophets attached to the cult, and functioning as cultic prophets.

All this would seem to set Israelite prophecy in a background of general Semitic prophecy, and to reduce the prophets of the Old Testament to a common stature with those of the surrounding peoples. In truth it but serves to bring out the uniqueness of Israelite prophecy the more. For if in its origin it was one with Semitic prophecy in general, in its achievement it far outstripped that of Israel's neighbours, and it alone produced anything of enduring value in the world. In so far as Israel's prophets were ecstatic, it is not because they were ecstatic that we are any longer interested in them, but because of the content of the oracles that came from their lips. In so far as Israel's prophets were cultic persons, it is not because they were attached to the cultus that we are interested in them, but because of the ethical and spiritual penetration of the message they proclaimed.

How far the prophets were ecstatic is disputed. Some writers would go so far as to claim that every oracle came to the prophet through some abnormal experience, which was its authentication for him and for his hearers, while others would give a lesser place to abnormality in their behaviour. How far the prophets were cultic persons is again disputed. Some would have all the prophets recognized as members of the personnel of the shrines, while others find some of the prophets to be of cultic status and others to be outside, and even opposed to, the cultus, while yet others deny that it is proper to speak of cultic prophets at all. But more fundamental is that essential quality of prophecy which makes it still relevant to the needs of men. And that lies in the nature of the prophet's work and in the content of his word.

The prophet claimed to be the mouthpiece of God, and his utterance was commonly introduced by the words "Thus saith Jehovah," or terminated with the words "Oracle of Jehovah." That there were varieties of prophet in Israel is quite certain. Not all lived in groups. Some were consulted in their own home, and some were found in the shrines. Some were attached to the court, either singly or in groups; and again some were found, both singly and in groups, exercising their function along the public roads. We find inner conflicts amongst the prophets, with mutual recriminations, each side calling the other false prophets. It is quite impossible to find any neat principles of distinction, or any rule of thumb, whereby we can distinguish the true from the false prophet. It is probable that all alike claimed to utter the word of God, and the same formulae probably marked their oracles. But not all proclaimed a message of equally enduring value for men, and the truth of the prophecy lay in the measure of its accord with the spirit of God. The uniqueness of Israel's prophecy lay in the unique spiritual quality of the message that so many of her prophets delivered, through forms and outer behaviour that differed so little from those of her neighbours.

Most of the oracles that have been preserved in the prophetic books are short, and cast in poetic form. Of the nature of Hebrew poetry something will be said below, but here it may be said that most of the prophetic oracles share precisely the same form that is found in the psalms. We doubtless have but a very small selection of the total number of oracles uttered by the prophets, and those we have are of varying worth or beauty. The pre-exilic prophets, speaking generally, are of far greater importance than the post exilic prophets, though the exilic prophet known as Deutero-Isaiah is second to none. Each has his own point of view, and his own especial message. It is a message to his contemporaries, and if it has any meaning for successive generations of men, it is not because it was primarily addressed to them, but because it was addressed to the prophet's own generation, and comes to others that yield to the same sins.

The message may have political or social significance, but that was never the primary significance. For the message of the prophets was religious, in so far as it was truly prophecy, and it proclaimed the will of God for men. The prophets perceived some elements of the Being and Nature of God, and implicit in their teaching was a theological message. Beyond this, they looked on the world in the light of what they had seen of God, and pronounced judgment on it accordingly, or proclaimed in advance the issue of the policies of their day, or called men to a truer obedience to the divine will. They were not always messengers of doom, but the pre-exilic canonical prophets were much more often messengers of doom than of peace. But that was because they found so little loyalty to God amongst those around them, and so little reflection of the quality of God's heart, as they perceived it, in the men of their day. For common to all the greater prophets of Israel was the recognition that whatever God was perceived to be, that they who worshipped Him should become, and all else but this was disloyalty to Him.

It will be seen that prediction is recognized in prophecy. Modern writers have so stressed the other elements in prophecy that sometimes they have given the impression that prediction was not even an element in prophecy. Certainly it was not the most important element, or almost the sole element, in the way some have supposed. Yet it cannot be denied a very real place in prophecy. But normally it was not prediction for its own sake, as a demonstration of the superhuman gift of the prophet, but prediction of the future as arising from the present addressed to their own contemporaries as a warning of the disasters to which they were heading, and closely connected with the profoundly spiritual message with which the prophet was charged.

In addition to this the prophets uttered predictions of the more distant future, not causally connected with their own times, when the Golden Age should dawn and life be incomparably beautiful. Despite all their dark forebodings, they were ultimately optimists. But their optimism was not based in man, or in the natural outcome of human policies, but in God, Whose will they believed would ultimately triumph, bringing perfect blessing to men. All this, however, was placed on the far horizons of time, with a hiatus separating it from the events of their own time and their immediate outcome.

The prophets, therefore, like the historians of Israel, were religious teachers, and it is as teachers of religious truth that they are to be judged. Indeed the work of many of them lay behind the work of the historians. For the book of Deuteronomy rested on prophetic teaching, and on its teaching rested the school that prepared all the books of the Former Prophets. The teaching of the eighth and seventh century prophets at least antedated the compilation of the historical books, though the books in which their own oracles were collected to be preserved in the Canon were not compiled until later.

CHAPTER IX

THE COMPILATION OF THE PROPHETIC BOOKS

THE canonical prophets are sometimes referred to as "the writing prophets," as though the earlier prophets left no written records of their work, while these prophets edited the books containing their oracles. This is completely misleading. In no case can we suppose that the prophet whose oracles are found in a book himself compiled the work, though we have evidence that one prophet, Jeremiah, did prepare a collection of his own oracles. That cannot be identified with the present book of Jeremiah, though it may well have formed one of the sources from which it was compiled.

There is evidence that there were once written records about some of the earlier prophets, and these must in some cases have preserved some of their oracles. It has been suggested above that the compiler of the books of Kings may have drawn on written works dealing with the prophets Elijah and Elisha, while the Chronicler refers to a work containing "the visions of Iddo the seer" (2 Chron. ix. 29), as well as to works containing the acts and oracles of Nathan and Ahijah of Shiloh (2 Chron. ix. 29). If these were extant at the time of the Chronicler, we can only wonder that they have not been preserved in the Canon.

The actual oracles of the prophets were probably in most cases very short, spontaneous utterances. This view, which has been most effectively advocated and applied by T. H. Robinson, has been opposed by J. Lindblom, who has argued for much longer units. In some cases the oracles were certainly of greater length, and we have in Isa. v. 1–7 an excellent instance of an oracle in three strophes, composed with great literary skill and artistry. The oriental memories, not alone of the prophets themselves, but of their hearers, and especially of their disciples, may well have retained them, and it is possible that some may have been written down almost immediately on ostraca. Ostraca were bits of broken pottery, which were used for various occasional purposes. The Lachish letters, that passed between a military garrison and its outposts, were written on ostraca, and it may well have been that just as we should use a scrap of paper to note down something that we wished to remember, a piece of broken pottery would be used to preserve an oracle. There would be no need to note the name of the speaker, and hence uncertainty could arise in a later day as to whose oracle the ostracon preserved. Hence we find some oracles ascribed to two different prophets, and hence, too, we probably have a number of oracles wrongly ascribed. Many oracles seem to be incomplete, and here again it may be because they were written on ostraca, which became further broken in course of time, before the oracles were gathered into collections.

In the case of Jeremiah, as has been said, we are told that at a certain point in his career he dictated a number of his past oracles to Baruch, who inscribed them on a roll and then read them in the Temple. The roll was subsequently taken to the king, and read in his presence, but the king, with supreme contempt, cut it off in strips and burnt it in the fire. Thereupon Jeremiah instructed Baruch to prepare a fresh roll, whereon he not merely wrote down again the oracles that had stood on the destroyed roll, but many more oracles were added unto them (Jer. xxxvi). Here we have evidence of something much less ephemeral than ostraca, but rather a definitely literary edition of some of Jeremiah's oracles. It was not a complete edition of all his oracles, for it was prepared in the middle of his career, and there is no evidence that it was kept up to date, and still less that it formed the present book of Jeremiah. If it had, then at least the later oracles would have stood in chronological order, whereas the arrangement of the book is not chronological.

Whether other prophets prepared collections of their own oracles we cannot know, but there is evidence that some of them did engage in some form of literary activity. For quite apart from the oracular poetry that stands in the prophetic books, we find some autobiographical material, usually in prose, though sometimes embodying brief poetic oracles that arose out of the incidents recorded in the prose. Examples of this are found in

Amos vii. 1–9, Hos. iii, Jer. xviii. Even here there can be no certainty that the prophet actually wrote down this autobiographical material himself. It may quite possibly have been spoken autobiography, which was written down at the time or subsequently by some hearer. This is suggested by the fragmentariness of the material of this kind that has come down to us.

There is, however, no reason to doubt that the author of the oracles and of the autobiographical material was the prophet himself, though we must not forget the certainty in some cases, and the probability or possibility in others, that a given oracle, while a genuine prophetic oracle of an unknown prophet, has been wrongly ascribed in the collection in which it stands.

Material of a third kind is found in the prophetic books. This is biographical material recorded in the third person, and again in prose, though in some cases embodying poetical oracles that were associated with the occasions dealt with. Here there is no reason to doubt that we have to do with memoirs of the prophets, prepared by disciples, either during their lifetime or, more probably, after their death.

Since the prophetical books of the Canon contain material of all these kinds we are clearly carried to a time much later than the prophet's own day for the compilation. We have to allow time for the literary collection of oracles, and for it to be forgotten in many cases who was the spokesman of a particular oracle, and even for much later oracles to be ascribed to a prophet. We have then to allow for a yet later stage, when material from the oracular collections, from the autobiographical collections, and from the biographical collections, was brought together. Nor must we omit to notice the evidence that our prophetical books rest sometimes on more than one collection of a prophet's oracles. Thus the little collection of oracles that stands in Isa. ii–iv has a separate heading, indicating that it once formed a separate collection. Probably the oracles in chap. i also formed a separate collection at one time. The compiler of the book wrote Isa. i. 1 as the introduction to the whole book, but although this rendered unnecessary the heading of ii. 1, he yet retained it.

We may next observe that there is evidence that the interest in collecting the prophetical books was a post-exilic interest. So far as the books of Jeremiah and Ezekiel are concerned, there can be no manner of doubt that they were not prepared until after the destruction of Jerusalem, since they contain stories of things that happened subsequently, and oracles from later times. Hence, if we allow time for the processes outlined above, we are carried down some time below this. It might seem, however, that so far as Amos, Hosea and Micah are concerned, to name no others, there is no reason to come down anything like so late. But here we should remember that the Minor Prophets do not consist of twelve books, but form a single compilation. That compilation contains oracles of pre-exilic and post-exilic prophets, and it was therefore not made until post-exilic days. It is probable that the collectors of this compilation worked directly with the materials of the various types above referred to, and not that they merely assembled books which had been already edited from these various materials.

It is therefore not surprising if the remaining work of the prophetic collection, the book of Isaiah, should prove to have been edited in the post-exilic age and to contain material long subsequent to the time of Isaiah of Jerusalem. For just as the four works that comprise the former Prophets were probably compiled within a relatively short space of time after the publication of Deuteronomy, so most probably the four collections that comprise the Latter Prophets were compiled within a relatively short space of time by circles that were interested in pre-exilic and post-exilic prophets alike. In that case we cannot place their work earlier than the latter part of the fifth century B.C., since it included the work of at least one fifth century prophet in the person of Malachi.

Here, as elsewhere, we must distinguish clearly between the age of the compilation of the books we now have and the age of the materials on which they draw. For here, as has been said, there is no reason whatever to doubt that a substantial amount of the material did actually come from the prophets whose names the various parts of the collection bear.

The method of compilation, however, is quite different from that of the books examined in the foregoing chapters. Here there is little in the way of framework, and as little in the way of a chronological sense. One would have expected the story of the call of the prophet to stand first, where it was recorded, and then at least to have had his early oracles before the later, even though strict chronology was no longer ascertainable. But the call of Isaiah is recorded in the sixth chapter of the book of Isaiah, and the only reference to the call of Amos stands in Amos vii, while chronological chaos marks more than one book. Often we have nothing whatever but internal contents to enable us to date an oracle, or to recover the circumstances that gave it birth. Sometimes the compiler seems to have strung his oracles together on a mnemonic principle, a word in one oracle helping to recall another oracle containing the same word, which immediately follows.

Thus, it is probable that Isa. i. 7 originally ended with the words "as the overthrow of Sodom," and in verse 9 we again find a reference to Sodom and Gomorrah. The oracle that begins in verse 10 may have been placed here because of its opening reference to Sodom and Gomorrah. Sometimes a series of oracles of perhaps widely varying dates seem to have been placed together because they have the same opening word. Thus in Isa. v we have a series of oracles that open with the word Woe! (vv. 8, 11, 18, 20, 21, 22). Again we often find a whole series of oracles on foreign nations collected together, as in Isa. xiii ff. Not seldom it is difficult to be sure when one oracle ends and another begins. The compilers seem to have had a profound regard for the prophets, and to have been willing to include anything that could present any claim to come from them, however fragmentary or however cryptic it was. Their work thus bears testimony to the high regard for the prophets, both pre-exilic and post-exilic, which marked the post-exilic circles to which the compilers belonged. This is in marked contrast to the lack of heed given to the pre-exilic canonical prophets in their own day.

CHAPTER X

THE BOOK OF ISAIAH

THE book of Isaiah stands first in the collection of the Latter Prophets, though Isaiah was not the earliest of the prophets whose oracles it contains. He received his call in the year that king Uzziah died (740 B.C.), whereas Amos preceded him by some twenty years. But nowhere does chronology seem to be of much interest to the compilers of these books, either in the order of the books in the collection, or in the order of the material within the books.

The book falls into two main divisions, of which the first, chaps. i–xxxix, deals mainly in judgment, and the second, chaps. xl–lxvi, deals mainly in consolation. Throughout the first part we find frequent mention of Isaiah's name, whereas in the second he is not once referred to. In the first part there is the mixture of biographical and autobiographical material with the oracles, while in the second we have nothing but oracles and some lyrical snatches. The background of the first part, with some exceptions, is Jerusalem in the Assyrian period, while that of the second is in part Babylon in the Chaldaean period, and in part Jerusalem without any reference to the conditions of the Assyrian period. It is not therefore surprising that almost all modern scholars treat chaps. i–xxxix quite separately from the chapters that follow, and find all the surviving work of Isaiah of Jerusalem within these chapters. By most scholars since the publication of Duhm's commentary in 1892, the remainder of the book is again divided into two, the chapters with the Babylonian background, xl–lv, being known as Deutero-Isaiah, while the remaining chapters, lvi–lxvi, which have a Judaean background, are known as Trito-Isaiah.

It will be most convenient, therefore, to consider each of these divisions of the book separately, though some modern writers have argued for the unity of chaps. xl–lxvi, and a very

much smaller number have argued for the ascription of the
oracles of the whole book to Isaiah of Jerusalem. The weakness
of this latter case is seen in the shifts to which its defenders are
put. Thus one recent writer holds that the teaching of the
second part of the book was handed down orally amongst the
disciples of Isaiah for a century and a half after his death, until
the period of the Babylonian exile, when a disciple edited the
prophecies of the first part of the book (i–xxxix), and wrote the
prophecies of the second (xl–lxvi), at the time when these
latter were being fulfilled. It is therefore recognized clearly
that these chapters as we now have them are of separate origin,
and they are only saved in some way for Isaiah by the vague
and gratuitous assumption of an oral transmission of formless
teaching.

(a) Chapters i–xxxix

Isaiah received his prophetic call in 740 B.C., and his
ministry continued at least until the end of the eighth century.
At the time of the Syro-Ephraimitish attack on Judah in 735–4
B.C. he delivered his message to king Ahaz in person, and during
the reign of Hezekiah he more than once took a prominent part
in events that can be specifically dated. He was opposed to the
anti-Assyrian coalition of 711 B.C., and again to that which
preceded the events of 701 B.C., when Sennacherib came
against the confederate states of the west, and broke the
rebellion. In the crisis of that year, however, Isaiah confidently
assured the king that Jerusalem itself should be spared, and his
word was vindicated when the Assyrians withdrew. We know,
therefore, something of the historical background of his work,
and we can place some of his oracles in the setting of this background. Others, however, are left with no sure setting.

The first chapter consists of several short oracles, particularly fragmentary at the end of the chapter, without any
indication of date beyond that supplied by their character.
On this ground some are ascribed to the crisis of 701 B.C. Chaps.
ii–iv form a little collection of undated oracles, of which the
first is ascribed independently to Micah (Mic. iv. 1–3). Chap.
vi contains the story of the prophet's call, while chaps. vii f.
carry us to the period of the Syro-Ephraimitish war. We cannot

assume that all the oracles in these chapters come from that period, but at least some can be securely linked with it. Chaps. ix–xi contain oracles with only internal evidence of date. Most of them can with confidence be ascribed to Isaiah, though the messianic oracles in ix. 2–7 and xi. 1–9 have been challenged by some, and xi. 10–16 is more generally regarded as non-Isaianic. Chap. xii has a character all its own in this book. It has not the appearance of a prophetic oracle, but is precisely similar to many of the psalms, and there is no reason to attribute it to Isaiah.

The next eleven chapters consist of oracles on foreign nations, similar to the collections of oracles on foreign nations found in Jeremiah and Ezekiel, and it is probable that some non-Isaianic material has found a place here. This material is perhaps drawn from a separate collection from the other collections of oracles used by the compiler, who had reason to believe that some of the oracles were Isaiah's, and then imported neighbouring oracles from the same collection into his work. The background of xiii. 1–xiv. 23 is clearly Babylonian, and it envisages Babylon as an imperial and ruthless power. This was not the situation in Isaiah's day, and when once it is recognized that the book contains some matter that did not issue from his, there seems no reason to claim this for him. It belongs rather to a later age, when Babylon was the mistress of the nations. It seems probable that this section is not a unity, but that xiv. 4b–23 is distinct from what precedes it. Similarly xxi. 1–10 comes from the exilic period, since it looks forward to the collapse of Babylon. While there are less obvious reasons for questioning other oracles of this part of the book, it is possible that some of them are not really Isaiah's, and they provide little positive ground for ascription to him.

The next section, xxiv–xxvii, is quite certainly not Isaianic. These chapters are totally different in outlook and in spirit from anything else in the book of Isaiah. They are wholly eschatological in character, and show more affinity with apocalyptic than with prophecy. That apocalyptic is the child of prophecy, and came into being by the one-sided development of certain elements in prophecy, is true. Yet apocalyptic is distinguishable from prophecy. By some writers this section of the book is held to be fully apocalyptic, while others find in it an approximation to apocalyptic, and a development from prophecy in the direction of apocalyptic. It does not show all the marks of apocalyptic, and especially it lacks the bizarre figures so characteristic of apocalyptic. Yet it shares with it one important feature.

The prophets addressed most of their exhortations to their contemporaries, and warned them of the issue of the policies on which they were embarked. But they also spoke of the Golden Age on the horizons of time. The apocalyptists believed that they stood near to those horizons, and that the Golden Age was about to dawn. They shared the prophetic view that that age was not causally connected with the events of their time, in the sense that it would be brought in by the labours of men. They believed it would come by divine intervention, but they believed that that intervention was about to take place, and the rule of righteousness that should last for ever about to be set up. These chapters of the book of Isaiah seem to envisage an imminent divine breaking into history and world judgment, and thus manifest an important feature of apocalyptic. But that feature is found in varying degree in other passages of the prophets, and has not a little in common with the popular conception of the Day of the Lord, of which we have evidence from the time of Amos (Amos v. 18). But whether we regard these chapters as fully apocalyptic or as an approximation to apocalyptic is of little moment. They are quite certainly of much later origin than the time of Isaiah, and are generally regarded as from the third century B.C., or, according to some, from the second century B.C.

Chaps. xxviii–xxxv consist of undated oracles, similar to those in the early chapters of the book, and some of them can with all confidence be accepted as Isaiah's, and in some cases be with probability set in the background of the events of 701 B.C. Yet here we find some elements that are probably of much later origin. Chaps. xxxiv f. seem to presuppose an exilic background at the earliest. Chap. xxxiv breathes a fierce hatred of Edom that reminds us of lxiii. 1–6, and that probably reflects the bitterness that was born of Edomite encroachment and cruelty during the period of the exile, while chap. xxxv promises the return of the Jews, and reminds us of passages in Deutero-Isaiah. Torrey, indeed, has argued that these two chapters belong to the second half of the book, and that the section xxxvi–xxxix was deliberately inserted after these chapters to dovetail the book securely together, and to ensure the connexion of Deutero-Isaiah with Proto-Isaiah.

Chaps. xxxvi–xxxix form a historical and biographical appendix, mainly duplicated in 2 Kings, though with the addition of the psalm of Hezekiah contained in xxxviii. 9–20. These chapters may have been taken from 2 Kings xviii–xx, or from the source whence the compiler of the books of Kings extracted them.

The first part of the book of Isaiah therefore contains much that cannot be ascribed to that prophet, and we are carried a long way below his time before it can have reached its present form. If the various collections on which the compiler drew already contained these non-Isaianic passages, we are certainly carried into the post-exilic age. And this seems more probable than that the work has been so extensively interpolated as we should have to suppose if we regarded all the non-Isaianic material as interpolated. If there were no major interpolations after the compilation of the work, we should have to place that compilation in the Greek period, since it is very improbable that the section Isa. xxiv–xxvii is earlier than the time of Alexander.

Many scholars believe, however, that this section has been added, and that the work of the compiler is to be placed in the middle of the fourth century B.C., towards the end of the Persian period. Others put the compiler somewhat later, and ascribe to him the preparation of the work in substantially its present form. Between these views only general probability can be our guide, but the present writer is not inclined to put the compilation of the books of the Prophetic Canon later than the middle of the fourth century B.C. While a theory of extensive interpolation after the compilation of the book is to be deprecated, the example of the appendix to the books of Samuel is evidence that some interpolation could take place.

Some elements of the teaching of Isaiah are common to him and to others of the pre-exilic prophets. These include his condemnation of the social evils of his day, and of the hollowness of the religiosity of his contemporaries, his perception that a nation that was wrong at its heart could not be right in its policies, and was bound to reap the fruits of its folly. Beyond these, there are some notes which are peculiarly his. In his call he perceived the holiness of God as something that was essentially ethical in its content. Before that holiness he was conscious not of his impotence or of his humanity but of his sin, and it was only the cleansing of his sin by the touch of the live coal that delivered him from the dread that he himself should be consumed with his sin (vi. 1–7). It was in the light of that holiness that he looked out upon the world and condemned the sin of men, a sin that consisted not so much in disobeying the word of God as in failing to reflect His moral glory.

Characteristic of Isaiah, too, is the doctrine of the Remnant, that was proclaimed in the name of his son, Shear-jashub (vii. 3). The disciplining of the nation would not wholly consume it, but would leave a Remnant to carry on its life and to inherit the promises (vi. 13, x. 20). He looked beyond the sorrows that were nigh to the distant hope, when the great Davidic leader should give to his people a reign of enduring righteousness and peace (ix. 2–7). His confidence that the power of God was great enough to protect Jerusalem from the boastful Assyrian, when men realized their own powerlessness and put their trust solely in Him, was vindicated, only to create in men of a later day a vain trust in the Temple as the guarantee of protection. Much earlier in his career, at the time of the Syro-Ephraimitish war, he had proclaimed the same fundamental message, that simple trust in God was more effective than any activity (vii. 3–9), but then he had not found a king who was ready to accept it. Nor is it likely that Isaiah would have held that trust in God without humble obedience to His will could be sincere. For his great denunciation of the sacrifices and ritual observances of his day (i. 11–17) was based on the fact that they were not the organ of the spirit of obedience to the will of God, and his great offer of cleansing and renewal (i. 18 f.) was conditional on that obedience.

(b) Chapters xl–lv

It has been already said that the background of these chapters is exilic, and the dominant note is of comfort and promise. The opening word is one of comfort and of assurance that the discipline of the nation is completed and deliverance at hand. In the course of the chapters we find the clear indication that Jerusalem is in ruins (xliv. 26, 28), and that the exile to Babylon has already been achieved (xlvii. 7). But now deliverance is at hand. Babylon will soon be overthrown (xlvii. 1–5, xlviii. 14), and the exiles will go forth (xlviii. 20, li. 11, lii. 11 f.), for Jerusalem and her people shall be delivered (lii. 1 f., liv). Nor is there any doubt as to the human agent through whom all this should be effected, for Cyrus is twice named (xliv. 28, xlv. 1). The sacred processions of Babylon are referred to (xlvi. 1 f.), probably by one who had witnessed the celebration of the New Year festival in that city.

In all this there is nothing to suggest the Isaiah of chaps. i–xxxix. It is true that we find certain phrases that were characteristic of him, including "the Holy One of Israel" (i. 4, v. 19, 24, x. 20, xvii. 7, xxix. 19, xxx. 11, 12, 15, xxxi. 1, xli. 14, 16, 20, xliii. 3, 14, xlv. 11, xlvii. 4, xlviii. 17, xlix. 7, liv. 5, lv. 5), but the whole tenor of the message and of the ideas that lie behind it, and especially the thought of God and its corollaries, are here different. Hence there can be no doubt whatever that here we have to do with an unknown prophet of the exilic period, who did his work in Babylon, and who heralded the return from the exile. This is agreed by almost all modern writers, though C. C. Torrey has argued that Isa. xxxiv f., xl–lxvi form a single work by a writer of *circa* 400 B.C., and has claimed that the references to Cyrus, Babylon and the Chaldaeans are interpolations in the text, whose removal leaves open the later ascription of the chapters. This view has secured little following, and is unlikely to do so.

In chaps. xlix–lv there is no reference to Cyrus, either direct or indirect, and instead of the clear Babylonian background some evidence of a Palestinian background has been alleged. Hence some writers have held that these chapters were written by the same author as xl–xlviii but somewhat later, and that the prophet was one of those who returned to Palestine when Cyrus gave permission. We should certainly expect that the prophet who had promised return would himself return when the opportunity arose, and there is thus some antecedent probability in this view. It is not universally shared, however, and it is to be noted that promises of return continue to stand in these chapters (li. 11, lii. 11 f., lv. 12 f.). It is therefore better to regard all these chapters as composed before the actual fall of Babylon. They may therefore be closely dated between *circa* 546 B.C. and 538 B.C.

The character of these chapters is quite different from that of the oracular portions of the earlier chapters of the book. There the oracles were normally short, and interspersed with some narrative passages. But here we have nothing but oracular material, interspersed with occasional lyrical songs, and the units are often much longer.

To certain passages special attention has been given in modern times. These are known as the Servant Songs. They are commonly held to consist of xlii. 1–4, xlix. 1–6, l. 4–9, and lii. 13–liii. 12. Some writers differently delimit these four songs, and some add other passages to them to make the number more than four. There is no agreement as to whether they are by the author of the surrounding passages, or whether they are earlier and incorporated by him from the start in his work, or later and interpolated into his work. Nor is there agreement as to whether they are to be interpreted as a connected series or whether they are to be interpreted each in relation to its own context, and therefore not necessarily alike. Perhaps the commonest view is that there are four songs, to be delimited as above, and that they were composed by the author of the rest of Deutero-Isaiah, but are to be interpreted as a series in relation to one another.

Traditionally the fourth of these songs was interpreted as a prophecy of Christ, but in modern times they have all been commonly interpreted of Israel. In the surrounding passages Israel is called the Servant of the Lord, and there are a number of links of phraseology between what is said about the servant in these passages, and what is said about Israel in the surrounding chapters. Yet the collective interpretation encounters some undeniable difficulties. So much so, indeed, that in the hands of some of its advocates it has been modified to mean the ideal Israel, or the Israel within Israel.

But from the days of Duhm there has been a tendency to

return to an individual view, though not of the older kind. Search has been made for a historical individual amongst the prophet's contemporaries or predecessors, of whom the songs could be interpreted, and the candidates for the honour of being the Servant have been legion. Moses, Uzziah, Jeremiah, Cyrus, Jehoiachin, an unknown contemporary of the prophet, Zerubbabel, and Meshullam the son of Zerubbabel, are amongst those who have found advocates, while Deutero-Isaiah himself has found not a few to support his claims. But here the difficulty lies in the fourth of the songs, in which the Servant's death and resurrection figure. Hence some have held that the fourth song was composed by a disciple of the prophet after his death. Recent advocates of the view that the songs are not to be interpreted as a series, but each in relation to its own context, have differed just as widely from one another when they have come to apply their principle.

It seems probable that no view will ever command general agreement. This may be because, as several writers have believed, there was some fluidity in the writer's thought, so that he would have had difficulty himself in defining with precision how he conceived the Servant. On this view the Servant was neither a collective figure nor an individual, but both. This view does justice to the links of phraseology with passages outside the songs, and also allows for the fact that in the fourth song, in particular, it is very hard to think that the writer had anything but an individual in mind.

On this view the Servant is Israel, yet narrowing down either to the true Israel, or to an individual who should be its representative, or in whom its mission should come to a focus, or who should carry that mission to a point no other should reach. Such fluidity is not uncommon in Hebrew thought. But in so far as the writer thought of an individual, it is unlikely that he believed that either he himself or any of his contemporaries or predecessors fulfilled the exalted role of the Servant. It would be some future individual who would give reality to his concept, and carry through the mission.

As to the nature of the mission, there is greater clarity. The first song declares that it is no less than the bringing forth of judgment to the Gentiles, by which he probably means the

carrying forth to the Gentiles of the true religion. The mission
is to be discharged in utter gentleness, linked with a persistence
that shall yield to no discouragement. The second song proclaims yet more clearly that the Servant is to be for a light to the
Gentiles, through whom the salvation of God shall embrace not
alone Israel, but the ends of the earth. The third song recog-
nizes that the mission will entail suffering for the Servant, while
the fourth perceives that the suffering will be the very organ
of the mission, in that through his suffering the Servant will be
perceived to serve those who inflict it on him, so that he will see
of the travail of his soul and fulfil his mission. Whoever the
Servant was in the thought of the writer, he was giving expression to great creative ideas, which have exercised a profound
influence on the world, and especially because of their influence
on Christ, in whom Christians have ever found the embodiment
of the prophet's thought.

Whether an individual Servant was the Servant *par ex-
cellence* or not, there are passages outside those noted above
where Deutero-Isaiah seems to have thought of the nation
Israel as called to a world mission, and this would seem to belong closely to some of his most characteristic ideas. No writer
attained so explicit and formulated a monotheism before him.
"Beside me there is no God" (xliv. 6) is a thought which is
frequently expressed in varying terms, and the utmost scorn
is expressed for the makers of idols, to which the prophet
allows no reality whatever. It is idle to reply that the makers of
idols were not worshipping the material of which the idol was
made, but the spirit that was believed to inhabit the material.
Since there was no God but Jehovah, who would have none
of idols, there was no god to inhabit the material, and therefore
the material was all that was left for the idolater to worship.

Moreover, no writer stressed so much the thought of the
divine election of Israel as this writer. Yet with fine insight he
accepted the corollaries of his thought. If God is one, then He
must be the god of all men, and not of Israel alone, and Israel's
election is not something to fill her with complacent pride, but
the basis of a mission to share her faith with all men. "Look
unto me and be ye saved, all the ends of the earth: for I am God,
and there is none else" (xlv. 22) is an utterance that clearly

bases his universalism on his monotheism; while "I the Lord have called thee in righteousness, and will hold thine hand, and will keep thee, and give thee for a covenant of the people, for a light of the Gentiles" (xlii. 6) relates the mission to the election.

(c) Chapters lvi–lxvi

In this final section we find ourselves in a definitely Palestinian *milieu* (lvii. 3–7), at a time when the Temple is standing (lvi. 5–7, lx. 7), though the walls of Jerusalem are not yet built (lx. 10). We are thus in the period between the Return and the time of Nehemiah. Some writers have held that Deutero-Isaiah is the author of these chapters, and that they were written in Palestine after the Return, and this view has found quite recent advocates. That Deutero-Isaiah may have continued to live for many years after the composition of Isa. xl–lv is perfectly credible, and there is certainly much in lvi–lxvi that reminds us of him. There are passages of great beauty and power that are fully worthy of his hand, such as lxi. 1–3. Yet beside them are others that fall far below the heights he attained, where the overwhelming sense of the glory of God is replaced rather by a sense of the glory of Israel.

Whereas in Deutero-Isaiah the glory of Israel lies in fulfilling the purpose of her election in making the only God known to all men, here her glory lies rather in the honour and service she receives from the nations (lxvi. 18–20). A more nationalistic spirit prevails, and there is fierce exultation in the thought of the vengeance that shall be exacted of Israel's foes (lxiii. 1–6), rather than the thought of a mission to be fulfilled in gentleness and suffering. There is still universalism, but the Gentiles are conceived of as coming to Jerusalem to show their sense of the sacredness of this spot (lvi. 6 f.), rather than in recognition that God is one. The externals of religion, such as the Sabbath (lvi. 2, 6, lviii. 13, lxvi. 23), and the Temple ritual (lvi. 7), come into the focus of interest.

It might be possible to argue that the exuberant spirit of Deutero-Isaiah had yielded to the withering effect of disappointment and disillusionment after he came to Palestine, and that the declension of his ideals was the consequence, but it

seems more satisfying to suppose, with most editors since Duhm
and Marti, that we have rather the failure of lesser men to reach
the heights of their master. The variety of levels reached in these
chapters is believed to be due to the fact that they come from
a variety of hands. The authors are believed to be men who
in varying ways and in varying degrees reflected the influence of
Deutero-Isaiah, and the composition of the whole is ascribed
to the period 520–450 B.C.

Not all scholars are agreed on this date, however. Abramow-
ski would allow a much wider range, 700–400 B.C., and Volz
somewhat similarly 600–400 B.C., while others would place the
composition rather later than has been suggested above. Pfeiffer
thinks of the period 450–350 B.C., and Torrey, as has been
noted above, *circa* 400 B.C., while Oesterley and Robinson would
assign some sections to a date as late as the latter half of the
fourth century B.C.

CHAPTER XI

THE BOOK OF JEREMIAH

THE problems of the book of Jeremiah are much simpler than those of the book of Isaiah. Here we find relatively little that cannot with confidence be connected with Jeremiah, though the stages by which the book reached its present form can only be conjectured. That Baruch's Roll formed one of the sources of the book has been agreed to be probable. This Roll is stated to have contained oracles, including some against foreign nations (xxxvi. 2), and it therefore may have constituted one of the collections on which the compiler drew. There is also biographical and autobiographical material in the book, though Mowinckel has suggested that the autobiographical passages were transcribed into the first person by the compiler, who took them from a source where they were originally in the third person.

The period covered by the ministry of Jeremiah was from 626 B.C. until shortly after the fall of Jerusalem in 586 B.C., and we have a much greater knowledge of the incidents of his life than we have of any other prophet. His book falls into four sections:

(*a*) chaps. i–xxv, consisting mainly of oracles from various dates, together with some prose matter, chiefly autobiographical;

(*b*) chaps. xxvi–xlv, consisting mainly of prose, both biographical and autobiographical, together with some oracles;

(*c*) chaps. xlvi–li, consisting of collected oracles against foreign nations;

(*d*) chap. lii, consisting of a historical appendix, which is duplicated in 2 Kings xxiv. 18–xxv. 21, 27–30, whence it was probably taken.

There are a few passages in the book which are generally agreed to be of later authorship. Thus x. 1–16 contains a polemic

against idols closely similar to those we find in Deutero-
Isaiah, and is quite un-Jeremianic in style. It is therefore
usually referred to the exilic age. Similarly l. 1–li. 58, which
prophesies the imminent fall of Babylon, is to be referred to the
same age, unless, with some, we regard it as a yet later imitation
of prophecy. Even later is xvii. 21–27, which recalls the age of
Nehemiah. Many scholars have denied chaps. xxx f. to Jeremiah,
but parts of them, and in particular the great passage on the
New Covenant (xxxi. 31–34), so well harmonize with the most
characteristic teachings of Jeremiah that we should be cautious
before adopting this view.

Nor have there been wanting scholars who have detected
a Deutero-Jeremiah. Volz regarded the oracles on the foreign
nations as the work of an anonymous prophet, writing soon after
the death of Nebuchadrezzar in 561 B.C. These prophecies
stand in a different place in the text of the Septuagint, where
they follow xxv. 13, and are found in a different order. They
may have been taken in the main from a separate collection
of oracles, but in view of the clear testimony contained elsewhere in the book that Jeremiah delivered oracles against
foreign nations, it is probable that some, at any rate, of these
oracles are his. Another recent writer would go to the other
extreme with the view that these oracles were all early oracles
of Jeremiah's, and that the prophet himself collected them.
Torrey, whose views are always original, has propounded
the view that Jer. i–x is a pseudepigraphic work of the third
century B.C.

With greater probability Mowinckel argued some years ago
that the collections of oracles drawn on by the compiler were
made between 580 B.C. and 450 B.C., while the autobiographical
prose work drawn on dates from about 450 B.C., and the biographical prose work somewhat earlier. While these dates for the
sources might perhaps be pushed back a little, it would be unsafe
to push them back more than a few decades.

In recent years a number of ostraca have been found on
what is believed to have been the site of the ancient Lachish,
and they contain references to a prophet, who has been identified
by some writers with Jeremiah. The evidence is quite insuffi-
cient to establish this, but the ostraca are valuable for their

confirmation of the conditions of the time, as reflected in the book of Jeremiah, and for their linguistic affinities with this book.

Apart from elements of his teaching shared with other prophets, Jeremiah is notable for his perception of the inner quality of religion as fellowship with God, depending not on this place or on that, but on the soul's *rapport* with God. The Temple was not essential to worship (vii. 1–15), nor was the true circumcision that of the flesh (iv. 4). His emphasis on the individual (xxxi. 30) is frequently noted, but he did not forget that the individual is a member of society, and in some way carried in the stream of its life. He warned men of the calamities their policies would entail for the children of his day (xvi. 3 f.), while denying that they could blame their fathers for their own sorrows (xxxi. 29). The formal inconsistency of these attitudes was due to his recognition of man's sociality and his individuality. The Covenant, to be valid, must be no mere inheritance from the past, but one the individual makes his own in the writing of its law on his very personality (xxxi. 31–34), though it should not be forgotten that it is still a covenant with the nation—with the house of Judah—and not merely with the individual. Jeremiah's teaching was born of his own experience of loneliness and suffering, and of a sensitiveness of spirit unsurpassed by that of any Old Testament figure we know. Unmarried, hated and persecuted by his own family (xi. 21–23), despised by Jehoiakim and bitterly hated by the courtiers of the weak Zedekiah, cast into a foul cistern (xxxviii. 6), he had scant human fellowship to sustain him. Add to this that the tarrying of the fulfilment of some of his prophecies made him a laughing-stock to men, and we can understand why there were times when he roundly vowed he would prophecy no more and complained that God had deceived him (xx. 7). Yet the prophetic fire, that could not be quenched, burned in his bones, and he was driven again to prophesy (xx. 9).

CHAPTER XII

THE BOOK OF EZEKIEL

A GENERATION ago the view that the book of Ezekiel was to be attributed wholly to the prophet-priest whose name it bears was almost unquestioned, but in the last twenty years it has found a long succession of challengers. The book falls into four main divisions:

(a) chaps. i–xxiv, containing prophecies delivered before the fall of Jerusalem, carefully dated and arranged in a chronological sequence;

(b) chaps. xxv–xxxii, containing prophecies on foreign peoples;

(c) chaps. xxxiii–xxxix, containing prophecies of the restoration of Jerusalem;

(d) chaps. xl–xlviii, containing an ideal sketch of the life of the restored community.

Ezekiel is presented as one of the exiles of 597 B.C., who exercised his ministry in Babylonia. He appears as a somewhat strange character, performing symbolic actions on a greater scale than any other prophet of whom we have record, and behaving with an eccentricity that is unique. His interest in the ritual of the Temple, and in priestly privilege, contrasts greatly with the lack of interest in these things shown by the pre-exilic prophets, for to Ezekiel the cultus was the focus of the national life. But whereas the pre-exilic prophets had condemned a cultus which was not the organ of the spirit, Ezekiel desired it to be purified of all idolatry and to be the organ of the spirit of the nation. He is often called the "Father of Judaism," and he is its father in its loyalty, as well as in its rigidity.

The problem of Ezekiel has now been lifted right out of this simplicity, however, and to-day there is no view on him which can claim any consensus of opinion. Hence all that can fairly be done here is to indicate briefly the variety of views that are held. Some views can with great probability be rejected. Here it may suffice to mention those of Hölscher, Torrey, Smith and Irwin. Hölscher started with the canon that Ezekiel could only write poetry, and so rejected as secondary almost all the prose—and some indeed of the poetry—in this book. He did allow the prophet a few verses of prose, indeed, but reduced the total of genuine matter in these forty-eight chapters to a mere 170 verses. The rest of the book was attributed to a fifth century editor. The arbitrariness of Hölscher's initial canon is a serious handicap to its acceptance.

Torrey maintained that the whole book is a pseudepigraph, written originally in the third century B.C., and purporting to be the work of a prophet of the time of Manasseh, but subsequently re-edited and transferred to the time of the exile. On Torrey's view, it was originally presented in a Palestinian setting, and this was changed to a Babylonian by its later editor. Almost simultaneously with Torrey's work appeared Smith's, who also connected the book with the age of Manasseh, but this time not as a pseudepigraph. Both Torrey and Smith find a fundamental unity running through the book, and both find an originally Palestinian background. Smith, however, places the writer in northern Israel, and thinks that chaps. xl–xlviii originally had reference to the sanctuary on Mt. Gerizim. Irwin claims to offer objective criteria for sifting the true from the false in this book, but he has convinced few of his fellow-workers and his results are almost as radical as Hölscher's. He rejects almost all interpretations of oracles, and accepts only poetic oracles as genuine, but allows Ezekiel some 250 verses.

Both Hölscher and Irwin deny the whole of chaps. xl–xlviii to Ezekiel. In this, though not in other respects, their view is shared by Herntrich, who also agrees with Torrey and Smith in the view that the background of Ezekiel's prophecies was Palestine. Herntrich does not remove Ezekiel from his ostensible age, but holds that he prophesied in Jerusalem until 586 B.C., and then in Babylonia. Later in the period of the exile, he argues, a disciple of the prophet's edited his work, and added much secondary material, including the whole of chaps.

xl–xlviii. This view of Herntrich's greatly influenced some other writers, including some British scholars.

Van den Born shares with Herntrich the view that Ezekiel's ministry began in Palestine and was continued in Babylonia after 586 B.C., when the prophet was deported thither. On the other hand, he accepts the substantial unity of the book, and assigns but minor passages to a glossator. He makes some substantial rearrangements of the book, however, and in particular transfers the inaugural vision of chap. i to follow chap. xxxii. It thus marks the opening of the Babylonian ministry. Auvray holds a similar general view, save that he assigns chap. xxxiii to the Palestinian ministry, and hence transfers chap. i to follow this chapter.

Bertholet places the call of Ezekiel in 585 B.C., and attributes to him a brief Palestinian period before his transfer to Babylonia, but thinks the book of Ezekiel was edited from notes left behind him in more than one version. He believed the editor transferred his work wholly to Babylonia and there interpolated it. Bertholet allows a considerable element of chaps. xl–xlviii to Ezekiel, however. Finally, we may note that Cooke returns much more nearly to the traditional view. He regards Ezekiel's ministry as exercised wholly in Babylonia, and finds a general unity running through the book. He does, however, find a number of expansions, including some in the concluding chapters.

From these views—chosen from a much larger number of recent works—it may be said that there is a widespread disposition to find some Palestinian matter in the genuine work of Ezekiel, and a general recognition that there is some secondary matter in the book, though estimates of its amount vary so widely. It is doubtful if chaps. xl–xlviii should be transferred bodily to another, even though he be regarded as a disciple. The present writer is doubtful if the book should be regarded as coming in its present form from a time anything like so early as the period of the exile. Its general lay-out is similar in some respects to that of proto-Isaiah and Jeremiah, save that there is no historical appendix duplicated from the book of Kings—for the sufficient reason that no relevant material stood in that book. This would suggest that the editing of this book was done in the same age as the others, and in the same circles. For the editing of the book we are thus brought down to the fifth or fourth century B.C. But here, as in the other books, the editor worked with sources containing oracles of the prophet, and the book is not to be thought of as a pseudepigraph.

CHAPTER XIII

THE BOOK OF THE TWELVE

THE twelve Minor Prophets are collected in what was a single compilation. The materials employed are probably of widely varying ages, since the periods of the prophets dealt with cover at least four centuries. It is probable that the books were edited for this collection directly from sources, and not merely collected as completed works. The problems of editing were different from those of the books so far considered, since the materials available were so much more scanty.

(a) Hosea

Hosea began his ministry at about the same time as Isaiah, but he seems to have completed it before the fall of Samaria in 721 B.C. He belonged to the northern kingdom and prophesied there, and it has been somewhat hazardously conjectured that he was a baker. We find the usual three types of material in his book, oracles in poetry, biographical prose and autobiographical prose. It would be difficult to suppose that three separate literary collections of material dealing with Hosea, yet so slight in their total volume, already existed, and we should perhaps think rather of notes, possibly on ostraca, than of formal literary sources.

In chap. i we have a biographical account of Hosea's marriage, while in chap. iii we have an autobiographical account of his relations with his wife. These chapters and their relation to one another, together with the whole question of Hosea's marriage, provide the thorniest problem of the book. The common view has been that the chapters supplement one another, chap. iii dealing with events subsequent to those of chap. i. The improbability of the one being taken from one source and the other from another in such a case has led some to suppose that the two chapters offer independent accounts

of the same events. Some have argued that Hosea married
two women, and that the two chapters are unrelated, and
some that the whole account of his marriage relations is
imaginary and symbolical. Vigorous defence of the faithfulness
of Gomer has been offered by some writers, while others feel
that it is fundamental to the experience of Hosea, and to the
message that was born of it, that his wife was unfaithful.

On the latter view, the prophet married a harlot—possibly
a temple prostitute—whom he profoundly loved, but who
was unfaithful to him, and he found in the bitterness of his
own experience and in his mingled love for his wife and
loathing for her sin a symbol of the love of God for the Israel
that was faithless to Him. His message was more profoundly
religious than that of his predecessor Amos, and he attacked
the Baalism that prevailed around him, and the sexual evils
that marked it, describing it as adultery and a breach of the
Covenant with God. He declared that God must discipline
Israel by disaster because He loved her, and sought to save
her from her degradation, but that He would not utterly destroy
her, even though she deserved it. All this, the fundamental
element of his message, seems to have been borne in on him
by the very depth of his domestic suffering.

Some editors have suspected of being later additions all
the hopeful passages of the book, but this seems unnecessary.
There is a note of hopefulness in xi. 8 f., which is certainly
from Hosea, and if chap. iii relates the sequel to chap. i,
there is a message of hope implicit also there. The passages in
which Judah is mentioned have with more probability been
suspected, though it is possible that the name Judah has
sometimes been substituted by a scribe for an original Israel
(so perhaps in xii. 2). It is generally agreed that i. 10–ii. 1 is
from another hand, but there is very little of this book which
need be denied to Hosea. It should be added that the text is
often corrupt, and particularly difficult.

(b) Joel

Nothing whatever is known about the prophet Joel, whose
name is given to this little book. In former days he was dated

in the pre-exilic period, either in the days of the minority of Joash, or in the time of Jeremiah. These views are generally abandoned for a post-exilic date to-day, though Kapelrud has argued for a date *circa* 600 B.C. The book falls into two parts:

(*a*) i. 1–ii. 27, dealing with a plague of locusts and the divine deliverance that followed repentance;

(*b*) ii. 28–iii. 21, dealing with the outpouring of God's spirit and the day of judgment.

The two parts of the work seem so different and unrelated that some recent writers hold them to be of independent origin, and the eschatological second part has been assigned to so late a date as the second century B.C. By others any strong reason for invoking two authors is denied, and it is held that the devastation of the locusts could well suggest to the prophet the Day of the Lord, when He would assemble the nations in the Valley of Jehoshaphat for judgment, and would grant blessing to the Jews.

The reasons advanced for holding the book to be post-exilic are:

(*a*) there is no reference to the northern kingdom, and Israel seems to be synonymous with Judah (ii. 27, iii. 2, 16);

(*b*) it is implied that the fall of Jerusalem is past and the Jews dispersed (iii. 2, 17);

(*c*) nevertheless the Temple—presumably the Second Temple—is in existence (i. 13 f.);

(*d*) the king is unmentioned, while the priests and elders seem to be the leaders of the land (i. 13 f., ii. 16 f.);

(*e*) there is no reference to Assyrians and Babylonians, but a reference to Greeks (iii. 6) would seem to carry us down to a later period;

(*f*) the sins denounced by the pre-exilic prophets do not figure here, while there is frequent mention of priests and sacrifices, and meetings for fasting and mourning (ii. 12), which suggests the attitude of post-exilic Judaism;

(*g*) the reference to the meal-offering and the drink-offering (i. 9, 13, ii. 14) brings us down to the post-exilic period.

Not all of these considerations are of equal weight, and some of them by themselves could easily be met. Nevertheless, there is a cumulative probability against a pre-exilic date.

There does not seem to be any reason, however, to come down below the latter part of the fifth century B.C. for the materials from which this book was compiled.

In recent years there has developed a tendency to study the prophets in terms of liturgies, and to find liturgical poems embodied in them. Amongst other such poems, some of which will be mentioned below, it has been claimed that Joel i. 1–ii. 27 should be included. That there were cultic prophets in Israel seems very probable, and it is possible that they composed poems for use in the ritual. Nevertheless, the present writer would view with extreme caution the proposal to find liturgical poems here. The primary known function of the prophets, whether true or false, whether cultic or non-cultic, was the delivery of oracles, and whatever amongst their work can be read as oracle is most naturally so to be read.

(c) Amos

Amos was the earliest of the prophets whose oracles have been preserved in the prophetic Canon. Himself a southerner, he delivered his message in the northern kingdom *circa* 760 B.C. He is frequently said by modern writers to repudiate the name of prophet (vii. 14, following R.V. marg.), but to the present writer this seems improbable. His words are more naturally to be rendered as in the text of R.V., and this view is reinforced not only by vii. 15, but also by iii. 7 f.

The book consists of the following parts:

(*a*) chaps. i f., containing seven oracles on the surrounding peoples, all introduced by a common formula, followed by a similar oracle on Israel;

(*b*) chaps. iii–vi, containing oracles denouncing the social evils of Israel;

(*c*) chaps. vii–ix, containing a series of visions, and some other biographical and oracular matter.

The three types of material found in so many of the prophetical books are found here, so that we are in any case carried well below the prophet's day for the compilation of the book. The genuineness of a few passages has been questioned. These include the oracle against Judah in ii. 4 f., and the concluding verses of the book, ix. 8b–15. The oracle against Judah is introduced by the same formula as the other oracles of the first two chapters, and it may have stood already in the collection from which they were taken. This would make the collection as late as the composition of these verses. The oracle that stands in ix. 11–15 appears to presuppose as its background a period not earlier than the exile, when the walls of Jerusalem were breached and the city was in ruins (ix.11), while ix. 8b–10, with its message of hope for the Remnant, stands in some contrast with ix. 1–4, which promises complete destruction with no word of hope. For the sources of the book we are therefore carried down to at least the exile, unless we assume that it has been subsequently interpolated. For its compilation we are therefore carried into the post-exilic age, with no precise *terminus ad quem*.

The message of Amos was one of fierce denunciation of the social evils of his day, and a cry for justice. The hollow splendour of the sacrifices of his day meant nothing, since righteousness was lacking in the life of the nation (v. 21–25). The extravagance of the upper classes (vi. 1–6) was sustained by the oppression of the poor (ii. 6, v. 11), and the processes of the courts, where verdicts were bought with bribes, were exploited for this purpose (v. 7, 12, 15, vi. 12). Yet it was not merely as an offence against man that Amos denounced these things, but as an offence against God, and against His election of Israel (iii. 2). For to Amos justice was of the very essence of God's Being, and therefore it must mark all who worship Him. Man's rights were his because God willed them for him, and God willed them for him because of what He was in Himself.

(d) Obadiah

This tiny book of twenty-one verses is in part duplicated in the book of Jeremiah (1–4 = Jer. xlix. 14–16; 5 f. = Jer. xlix. 9, 10a). It is probable that the duplicated verses belong to their context here, and were wrongly ascribed to Jeremiah. We know nothing about the prophet, save what can be gleaned from these few verses, and it is disputed whether even all of these come from a single prophet.

The contents of the book are:

(*a*) verses 1–14, containing a denunciation of Edom;

(*b*) verses 15–21, containing a prediction of the coming Day of the Lord, when Edom would be wiped off the face of the earth.

Both parts of the book are strongly nationalistic, and there is nothing of the higher message of prophecy here. There is rather an earnest cry for vengeance, and a passionate exultation in the thought of its exaction. It is clear from verse 11 that the destruction of Jerusalem is already past, and this is confirmed by the general attitude towards Edom, which is shared by Isa. xxxiv, and lxiii. 1–6. All of these passages probably reflect the bitterness felt towards Edom for the help she had given the Chaldaean enemy (2 Kings xxiv. 2—where we should read Edomites for Syrians), and her joy at the sorrows of her neighbours (Lam. iv. 21), as well as for her cruel pressure during the period of the exile.

There would seem to be nothing here that could not come from the mouth of a prophet of the exilic period, living still in Palestine, and Rudolph would ascribe the whole to one author, with the possible exception of the last three verses. Other writers, however, parcel the book out amongst various authors, of widely separated ages. Thus Sellin ascribes vv. 1–10 to a ninth-century prophet, vv. 11–14 to an exilic author, and vv.15–21 to a fifth-century contemporary of the prophet Malachi, while Pfeiffer attributes vv. 1–14 to a contemporary of Malachi, vv. 16–18 to a writer some half-century later, *circa* 400 B.C., and vv. 19–21 to one who lived in the first part of the fourth century B.C.

(*e*) *Jonah*

The book of Jonah contains no oracles, and consists throughout of biographical prose, save for the psalm in chap. ii. We know nothing of the author, who is not to be confused with Jonah, the son of Amittai, mentioned in 2 Kings xiv. 25. It has been improbably suggested that the book of Jonah once formed part of the book of Kings, where it followed 2 Kings xiv. 27. It was probably a story composed about the Jonah of 2 Kings xiv. 25, but composed long after his time.

Whether it contains any historical kernel cannot be known. Sellin thought the mission of Jonah to Nineveh might be historical, and compared that of Elijah to Damascus. But that the story has been embellished with legendary material Sellin was fully persuaded. The obstacles to the acceptance of the historicity of the story include much greater difficulties than the story of the fish. The city of Nineveh is described as a city of three days' journey (iii. 3), by which the following verse makes it clear that the writer means a city that it would take three days to pass through. But the walls of the city measured less than eight miles in circumference, and its area was less than three square miles. The estimate of its population (iv. 11) is therefore similarly grossly exaggerated. Moreover, its king is not called the king of Nineveh in any contemporary texts, or elsewhere in the Old Testament. That Nineveh was instantaneously converted is a thesis which will not convince any students of her history, unless the conversion was as ephemeral as it was swift—in which case it was worthless, and hardly likely to deceive God.

It is clear from iii. 3 that the days of Nineveh, which was destroyed in 612 B.C., were long past when this book was written, and linguistic considerations reinforce this with their evidence of post-exilic date. Pfeiffer believes the author was acquainted with the book of Joel, which he dates about 350 B.C., and claims that the writer's views on repentance through fasting and sackcloth, leading to divine forgiveness, were derived from Joel i. 13 f., ii. 13 f. With the earlier dating of Joel suggested above, the date might be pushed back somewhat, but it is improbable that we should place the book of Jonah earlier than the fourth century B.C.

While the book of Jonah contains no prophetic oracles, it delivers through the medium of its story a prophetic message, and the historicity of the story is no more necessary to the validity of the message than was the historicity of Nathan's parable (2 Sam. xii. 1–4) to the validity of his. Jonah stands for the Jews. He was swallowed by the fish for his disobedience, and they swallowed in the exile for their disobedience; he was vomited to fulfil his mission of converting the heathen, and they were restored to lead the nations to God.

Here is a prophetic message which is closer to some elements of the teaching of Deutero-Isaiah than we can find anywhere else in the prophetic Canon. For here the missionary interest is completely freed from any trace of Jewish nationalism, and is born of a spirit of compassion for men that is supremely unselfish. It is probable that in Jonah's reluctance to undertake his mission we should see reflected something of the author's spiritual pilgrimage, and his reluctance to believe the message he was commissioned to deliver.

The psalm in ii. 2–9 has no real relevance to its context, and is probably of independent origin, though Aalders has contested this view. It is a song of thanksgiving for some deliverance at sea, and not a prayer for deliverance, such as its heading proclaims it to be. Doubtless the compiler placed it here because Jonah's plight reminded him of that from which the singer had been saved.

(f) Micah

With Micah we return to an eighth-century prophet, who was a Judaean contemporary of Isaiah. He is referred to in Jer. xxvi. 18, where Mic. iii. 12 is inexactly cited as the utterance of a prophet of Hezekiah's days. Unlike the book of Jonah, which contains no oracles, this book contains only oracles and we have no knowledge of the prophet.

The book consists of three parts:

(a) chaps. i–iii, denouncing the social evils of Judah, and ending with the prophecy of doom, cited in Jeremiah;

(b) chaps. iv f., offering promises of restoration;

(c) chaps. vi f., containing miscellaneous oracles.

That the first three chapters are the genuine oracles of Micah is agreed by all. The evils there denounced are similar to those denounced by Isaiah, but there is a note of bitterness in Micah that has suggested to editors that the prophet had suffered the things of which he complained. The only notable thing about his message is his anticipation by a century of Jeremiah's prediction that the Temple should be destroyed.

The rest of the book is commonly denied to Micah. The oracle which stands in iv. 1–4 is duplicated in Isa. ii. 1–3, but

here an extra verse is added. In the rest of chaps. iv f. there
are some indications of an exilic or post-exilic date, that must
either be deleted as glosses, or allowed to prove that the
oracles come from a later date. In chaps. vi f. there is material
which might be from Micah, though there is little positive
reason for saying that it is. On the other hand, the great passage
denouncing child sacrifices (vi. 6–8), one of the greatest passages
in the prophetic Canon, is generally denied to him.

The evil it denounces is known to have flourished in the
days of Manasseh, and hence it is believed that this oracle
dates from that reign. With less probability some have argued
for the reign of Ahaz. That Micah might have lived on into
the reign of Manasseh is possible, though the fact that the
heading of the book (i. 1), does not mention this reign is against
it. Of greater weight is the consideration that in spirit and tem-
per this oracle differs greatly from those of the first three
chapters. Yet even here Micah would not be the only person
to utter a mellower message many years after he had struck a
more rasping note. Hence the present writer is not inclined
to pronounce for or against Micah's authorship. Its noble
teaching is of more consequence than its authorship.

The final passage, vii. 2–20, is commonly assigned to the
period of the exile, or later. Gunkel has argued that part of
this consists of a liturgy, in line with the tendency above noted
to find liturgies in the prophetic books.

(g) Nahum

The prophet Nahum can be dated only on internal evidence,
since the title does not indicate the reigns in which he lived.
That he prophesied before the fall of Nineveh in 612 B.C. has
been generally agreed, since he prophesied of that event. On
the other hand, he looks back on the sack of Thebes (663 B.C.)
in iii. 8. These are the only certain termini available to us.
However, the fierce glee with which he hails the coming fall
of Nineveh would suggest that he prophesied very close to
that event.

The book opens with a mutilated acrostic poem (i. 2–ii. 2),
which is generally held to be of quite independent origin, and

to come from post-exilic times. The oracles of Nahum then follow in ii. 3–iii. 19. But Humbert has applied the liturgical principle to the study of the whole book, and argued that it was written, not before the fall of Nineveh, but just after that event, to be liturgically used at the festival that celebrated the fall of the proud city. Haldar rejects this theory, but holds that the book comes from a cultic prophet, and that it was a piece of political propaganda against Nineveh, modelled upon the cultic myth of Jehovah's victory over His foes.

Of the brilliance of the writing of Nahum there can be no doubt, but of the loftiness of his prophetic message there is greater doubt. Some writers class Nahum with the false prophets, who stood opposed to the great prophets of judgment. He delivers no spiritual call to his own people, but merely exults in the terrible scenes which he pictures as taking place in Nineveh. It is easier for us to condemn him from this distance than it might have been if we had suffered under Assyrian cruelty, and it should not be forgotten that even an Isaiah, who believed that Assyria was the rod of Jehovah's anger, predicted with some relish that she would yet be destroyed when she had served His purpose (Isa. x. 12–15). Isaiah had no love for Assyria, and would have known no tenderness for her in the hour of her downfall. Yet, when this is said, it remains true that Nahum had no word of spiritual penetration, and he contrasts greatly with his contemporary Jeremiah. Moreover, the fall of Nineveh, which he hailed, brought no relief to Judah, for another yoke was promptly fastened on her, and within a few years she suffered more severely under the new power than she had ever suffered under Assyria.

(h) Habakkuk

The prophet whose oracles are preserved in the book of Habakkuk apparently belonged to the Chaldaean period. In that case he was a contemporary of Jeremiah. Not all the book consists of his oracles, however, for it falls into two parts:

(a) chaps. i f., consisting of oracles, at first against Judah, and announcing the rise of the Chaldaeans for the discipline of the wicked oppressors, and then against unspecified oppressors;

(b) chap. iii, consisting of a psalm, precisely like many of the psalms in the Psalter. The heading "Shigionoth" recalls the heading of Ps. vii, while the note at the end, "For the Chief Musician, on stringed instruments," is paralleled in the headings of several psalms. Moreover, the term Selah stands three times here (iii. 3, 9, 13), and nowhere else outside the Psalter.

So far as the first two chapters are concerned, Cannon finds no reason to doubt that they preserved the oracles of a seventh-century prophet, who first heralded the coming of the Chaldaeans, just as Isaiah had heralded the coming of the Assyrians, as the instrument in God's hands to purge His people, but who later, after some experience of Chaldaean cruelty, prophesied against them.

Many scholars have rejected this view of the chapters, however, and diverse views on them have been held. Budde dated the prophecy circa 615 B.C., and ascribed it all to one author, but found only an anti-Assyrian attitude revealed in it. Others divide the oracles between two writers, dating the one circa 605 B.C., and the other during the exile, or find the original work of Habakkuk to be much interpolated.

A more radical treatment was proposed by Duhm, who suggested the reading Kittim for Kasdim in i. 6, and hay⁣ʿwāni (= the Greek) for hayyayin (= wine) in ii. 5, and then transferred the whole prophecy to the Greek period, and to the time of Alexander. Torrey has followed this view, but the only evidence for it lies in the emendations which are dictated by it, and these clearly have no independent evidential value.

Once more a liturgical view has been proposed. This was advanced by Balla, and it has been adopted by Sellin and Humbert. According to Humbert, Habakkuk was a cultic prophet of the closing years of the seventh century B.C., in whom we find a synthesis of prophetic ideas and of cultic loyalty. He differs from Cannon in finding a greater unity of time and of theme in the chapters, holding the oppressor throughout to be Jehoiakim. On the liturgical view, Sellin suggested that it was composed for a day of prayer at the time of the Chaldaean peril, and Humbert dates it precisely in 602–601 B.C.

Duhm regarded the psalm as integral to the book, and on the liturgical view it can be accepted as the closing hymn of the liturgy. But others regard it as of quite independent origin, and ascribe it to the post-exilic age. On general grounds the cultic view is to be treated with caution, and on every ground the view of Duhm is to be rejected. The psalm appears to be taken from a collection of psalms, such as can with difficulty be assigned to the pre-exilic period. But the rest of the book can with all probability be assigned to the end of the seventh century B.C., though the precise reference of every oracle cannot be decided with certainty.

The prophet is of some importance because he raised the question of the suffering of the righteous at the hands of the unrighteous as a speculative, and not merely as a practical, problem (i. 13), and also because he attained the thought that "the just shall live by his faith" (ii. 4). This was taken up into the New Testament and into Reformation thought, where it was re-applied in ways of which Habakkuk can little have dreamed.

(i) Zephaniah

The prophet Zephaniah prophesied in the reign of King Josiah, probably at the time of the Scythian peril in 626 B.C., when Jeremiah received his call[1]. The lineage of Zephaniah is given to the fourth remove, and is traced to Hezekiah (i. 1), and it may be because this was King Hezekiah that we have this unusual fullness. Like Jeremiah, at the outset of his career, Zephaniah seems to have believed that the approach of the Scythians heralded general disaster, but whereas Jeremiah seems to have thought only of his own people, Zephaniah thought of a widespread judgment on the nations. The popular idea of the Day of Jehovah as a day of divine deliverance for Israel and vengeance on her foes, had been rejected by Amos, who declared that it would be a day of darkness and not

[1] Many scholars deny that there was any Scythian peril at this time, and would dismiss the whole "Scythian hypothesis" as irrelevant to the study of Jeremiah or Zephaniah.

light (Amos v. 18). Extending this thought, Zephaniah thinks of it as a day of universal darkness and judgment.

Although the book is so small, there is no need to suppose it all belongs to a single point of time. If the view is correct that the prophetic oracles were normally very short utterances, we may have many separate and distinct oracles here, and though relatively few have come down to us, we have no reason to doubt that Zephaniah's prophetic ministry may have covered several years. Hence when we find in ii. 13–15 a prediction of the destruction of Nineveh, we have not necessarily to carry the whole book down to the date of Nahum's oracles. Indeed, since the revolt of Babylon under Nabopolassar against Assyria was almost synchronous with the call of Jeremiah and the Scythian peril, and since the reform of Josiah in 621 B.C. was probably the religious side of a parallel revolt in Judah, it is not at all improbable that a Hebrew prophet might hail the coming downfall of Assyria long before Nineveh actually fell.

Some scholars have rejected a few verses as later additions, and some have found more extensive additions. Thus, Pfeiffer holds that little, if anything, in chap. iii can be credited to Zephaniah. Sellin, however, upholds the genuineness of almost the whole of this chapter.

(j) Haggai

In the book of Haggai we have exactly dated oracles, whose dates there is no reason whatever to doubt. It contains but two chapters, yet we have several addresses, and all fall within a single year. This was the second year of Darius Hystaspis (520 B.C.), when the work of building the Second Temple was begun.

Unlike the pre-exilic prophets, who had so often denounced the sacrifices of their own day, and Jeremiah in particular, who had predicted the destruction of the Temple, Haggai was wholly concerned with the rebuilding of the Temple and the restoration of the sacrifices. The formal contrast with the pre-exilic prophets should not be exaggerated, however, for it is unlikely that they would have approved of the religious deadness of Haggai's day. The pre-exilic prophets declared

that the forms of religion without the substance were meaning-
less, since it was the substance that gave meaning to the forms,
while the post-exilic prophets rather urged that where there
was the substance of religion it must express itself in the forms.
Nevertheless, it is rather for its historical value than for its
religious importance that this book is esteemed.

The prophet is consistently referred to in the third person,
and it is therefore probable that the actual compilation of the
material of this book was done by another hand. There are,
however, those who think that it is to be ascribed to Haggai
himself, but that he studiously referred to himself in the third
person. In any case, there is nothing here that could not have
been written down very soon after 520 B.C., and the compiler of
the Book of the Twelve does not seem to have added anything
to it, but to have taken it wholly from a homogeneous source.

(k) Zechariah

If the book of Haggai is homogeneous, the same cannot be
said of the book of Zechariah. For here it is generally agreed
that we have a composite work, which falls into two main
divisions:

(a) chaps. i–viii, containing the prophecies of Zechariah;
(b) chaps. ix–xiv, containing the work of a later writer
of the apocalyptic school.

So far as the first section is concerned, we have carefully
dated prophecies of a contemporary of Haggai's, who was
equally concerned with him in the rebuilding of the Temple
and the renewing of the nation's life. The dated material
ranges from 520 B.C. to 518 B.C., and consists of eight Night
Visions. These are all related in the first person, but the
headings (i. 1, 7, vii. 1) are in the third person. These visions
all centre in Zerubbabel, until he disappears, and attach to
him messianic hopes. For the background of these hopes we
should recall that on the death of Cambyses pseudo-Smerdis
claimed the Persian throne, while there was a general revolt of
all the empire, which seemed likely to break up into separate
units. In such a situation it would not be surprising for the
hope to be cherished in Judah that freedom was once more to

be had, and a fresh start to be made in the life of the nation under a restored Davidic leader. But Darius Hystaspis assumed the lead, and reduced the provinces one by one to submission again, and the dream of freedom vanished. It is possible that Zerubbabel was eliminated because of the hopes that had centred in him, and that the two crowns of vi. 11 were really designed for Zerubbabel and Joshua, though they are now represented as both for the head of Joshua, the high priest.

The rest of the book presents greater problems. It is separated from the earlier chapters for a variety of reasons:

(*a*) there is no indication of the Persian period as the background of these chapters, whereas such a background is clear and explicit for the earlier chapters;

(*b*) here we find Jerusalem at war and besieged, whereas in the earlier chapters she was at peace and the Temple being rebuilt;

(*c*) the leaders of the community are here unnamed shepherds, whereas in the earlier chapters they were Zerubbabel and Joshua;

(*d*) the theological ideas here appear to be other than those which mark the earlier chapters;

(*e*) literary considerations of language and style favour separate authorship.

As to the identifying of the period from which these chapters came, the problem is much harder. If the precise reference of the "shepherds" were known, it would be much easier. The general character of these chapters approximates to apocalyptic, and at the same time there are indications of the currency of the priestly law. There is emphasis on the ritual observances (xiv. 16–21), and prophecy is so discredited that it is regarded as inconceivable that another true prophet should arise (xiii. 2–6). All of this would seem to carry us to the late post-exilic period, and the reference to Greece in ix. 14 well agrees with this. By many scholars the chapters are dated in the third century B.C., and by some as late as the second century B.C. The latter is highly improbable, and if the former is correct, we should have to regard these chapters as added to the collection of the Minor Prophets after the work of the general editor was complete.

By some scholars these chapters are not regarded as a unity, and a pre-exilic date has been proposed for part of them. Thus Steuernagel held chaps. ix–xi to be pre-exilic, while chaps. xii–xiv were post-exilic. Perhaps the most complicated view is that of Oesterley and Robinson, who make a sevenfold division of chaps. ix–xiv, and ascribe them to dates that range from shortly before 200 B.C. to after 134 B.C. This would make the work of the editor who gathered these various fragments together and inserted them into the text too late to be probable.

(*l*) *Malachi*

Whether Malachi, which means *My Messenger*, is a proper name at all is disputed, but is of little moment. In any case we know nothing of the life of the prophet, though we know his date with reasonable certainty. That date is shortly before the time of Nehemiah, perhaps *circa* 460 B.C.

The grounds on which this view rests are:

(*a*) the land is ruled by a governor (i. 8), and so the time, is after the destruction of Jerusalem;

(*b*) nevertheless the Temple is standing (i. 10, iii. 1, 10), and it is therefore after 516 B.C.;

(*c*) no distinction is made between priests and Levites (ii. 4–9, iii. 3), and therefore the Priestly Code has not yet been promulgated;

(*d*) the condemnation of mixed marriages (ii. 10–16), suggests that Nehemiah's measures to deal with this problem had not yet been undertaken (cf. Neh. xiii. 23–27).

There is one point which might suggest that the book is later than the issue of the Priestly Code. This is the agreement of iii. 10 with P's tithe law (Num. xviii. 21–23), as against D's (Deut. xiv. 22–29). It is possible that the practice is older than the codification of P, in accordance with the principle noted above that all the provisions of a new code are not themselves necessarily new.

Malachi's message, like that of other post-exilic prophets, is of the necessity to take the cultus seriously, and to bring worthy offerings to the Temple. He finds the vitality of the

religious life threatened by mixed marriages and by indiffer-
ence, and the best justification for the work of Nehemiah and
Ezra, and for the establishment of Judaism, with the new
dangers it brought in its train, is to be seen in the picture
this book sets before us.

The general editor of the whole Book of the Twelve is
doubtless responsible for the closing verses of Malachi, which
are intended not so much to close this book as to close the
whole prophetic collection. He believed that prophecy had
now come to an end, and that henceforth the written direction
of the law of Moses was to replace the living direction of the
prophets' word.

BOOK IV
THE WRITINGS

CHAPTER XIV

THE CHARACTER OF HEBREW POETRY

THE first three books of the last division of the Hebrew Canon are referred to as "the poetical books." It is only in modern times that the forms of Hebrew poetry have been seriously studied, and its principles recovered, after having been lost for centuries. Much is still far from clear, but some things are reasonably certain. And amongst them is the fact that Hebrew poetry is by no means confined to the three books referred to, together with a few expressly recognized poetical passages elsewhere, such as the Song of Moses (Deut. xxxii). Much that stands in the prophetical books is of precisely the same form, and much in books that stand outside the Canon shares the same form. Nor is that form limited to Hebrew poetry. Babylonian poetry has the same marks, which are also found in Ras Shamra texts that have so recently come to light. Hence Hebrew poetry stands to-day in a background of Oriental poetry much wider than used earlier to be thought.

Rhyme marks Hebrew poetry only in a most rudimentary and occasional way, if at all, and was certainly no essential in Old Testament times. Parallelism and rhythm, however, appear to be much more essential forms.

By parallelism it is meant that the unit is normally not the single line, but the balanced couplet, with a definite pause in the sense at the end of the couplet, and a lighter caesura in the middle of the couplet. Sometimes, however, a triplet stands instead of a couplet, to form still a single unit of the poem. In parallelism is no dull monotony, for it may be either *synonymous*, where the lines reinforce one another (e.g., Ps. xviii. 5), or *antithetical*, where they stand in contrast (e.g., Ps. xxxiv. 10), or *synthetic*, where there may be a parallelism of form, or a less defined parallelism of idea (e.g., Ps. xxvii. 4). Further refinements of parallelism are *emblematic*, where the second line is a simile illustrating the thought of the first (e.g., Ps. cxxix. 5 f.), *stairlike*, where part of the first line is repeated and the thought then carried forward (e.g., Ps. xcvi. 7), or *introverted*, where the first line is parallel to the fourth of a quatrain instead of to its successor, while the intervening lines are parallel (e.g., Ps. cxxxvii. 5 f.).

An independent and quite different analysis of parallelism is that of Buchanan Gray, who distinguished complete parallelism from incomplete. With *complete* every term of the one line has its counterpart in the other (e.g., Isa. li. 6), while with *incomplete* some term or terms in the first line cannot be paralleled in the second. Here we may find either that there is *compensation*, i.e., something new in the second line replaces what is not paralleled, or two terms in the second line correspond to but one in the first (e.g., Judges v. 4), or *no compensation*, where everything in the second line is paralleled in the first, but not everything in the first is paralleled in the second (e.g., Isa. i. 6).

All of these can be appreciated in a translation, provided it is remembered that a single word in Hebrew often stands for more than one word in English. The further way of securing variety in the Hebrew by varying the order of paralleled words is less easily appreciated in translation.

The rhythm of the Hebrew can often be felt in translation, though it is not always easy to bring out. For Hebrew rhythm is counted by significant words. Normally each word conveys a significant idea, and counts as a single unit of the line. But a single particle may not be separately reckoned, or two short words closely linked together in a genitive relation may reckon as one, while, on the contrary, a long word may reckon as two units. Hard and fast rules as to when two short words reckon as one, or one long word reckons as two, cannot be laid down.

The commonest rhythms are 3 : 3 and 3 : 2, but as has been said above a triplet may take the place of a couplet, and with the second of these rhythms the additional line may be either a line of three units, standing first or last, or a line of two units, standing last. A poem which is dominantly of either of these rhythms need not necessarily conform invariably to this pattern. We may find that by catalexis either half is truncated

by one unit, or both, save that with 3 : 2 rhythm the second
half would not be truncated. On the other hand, we may
find that by hypercatalexis either half is extended by one
unit, or both, and it frequently happens that at the end of a
poem we have a weighted couplet, with each half extended,
or a triplet taking the place of a couplet. A further form of
variety is found with 3 : 3 rhythm. This is the introduction
of a double caesura, giving 2 : 2 : 2. Moreover, introductory
words of poems, or of sections of poems, may stand by ana-
crusis outside the rhythmical scheme.

The division of poems into stanzas of greater measure than
the individual couplet is not general in Hebrew poetry, though
there are a number of poems which are clearly strophic.

In modern works considerations of parallelism and rhythm
are frequently invoked to justify emendation of the text.
Rarely do these considerations alone justify any change of
the text, but they certainly provide a most valuable reinforcing
consideration where we have any other evidence for emending
the text. One of the clearest instances is Amos vi. 12, where
R.V. has "Shall horses run upon the rock? will one plow
there with oxen?" The word "there" is absent from the Hebrew,
as R.V. shows by italics. Yet if it is omitted, the verse is
reduced to nonsense. The first half is a rhetorical question,
expecting the answer "No," and something similar is expected
in the second half. The word rendered "oxen" is unique in
the Old Testament, in that it is the plural of a collective term.
Further, the rhythm of the context leads us to expect 3 : 3
here, whereas we find 3 : 2. This could be a case of catalexis,
but if we divide the word rendered "oxen" into two, separating its plural termination to form a separate word, we get
the meaning, "Or doth one plough *the sea* with oxen?"
Normal grammar, sense and rhythm are all thus restored, and
parallelism is enriched.

While this simple statement is necessarily very incomplete,
it may enable the reader to appreciate the frequent references
to metre in the commentaries, and perhaps to appreciate both
the use and the limitations of metric considerations.

CHAPTER XV

THE PSALMS

OF few books has the study been more transformed during the present century than the Psalter. At the beginning of the century scholars were largely interested in determining the precise date of each of the poems, and the circumstances out of which it arose, and the general tendency was in the direction of late dating. Almost all the psalms were ascribed to the post-exilic period, and very large numbers to the Maccabaean age. To-day there is less effort to fix precise dates, but a general tendency towards earlier dating. It is commonly allowed that there may be a considerable pre-exilic element in the Psalter, and in some quarters there is a reluctance to find more than the slightest post-exilic element. Moreover, altogether new lines of study have opened up.

The Psalter consists of 150 poems, divided into five books (i–xli; xlii–lxxii; lxxiii–lxxxix; xc–cvi; cvii–cl). This division was probably in imitation of the Pentateuch, but it is generally believed that an earlier division was into three books. In several cases we appear to have two separate psalms combined in one (e.g., Ps. xix, where vv. 1–6 and 7–14 are separate, the latter reminding us of Ps. cxix in its character), while in some cases one psalm has been divided into two (e.g., ix and x, shown to be one by the alphabetic arrangement and the lack of heading for x; and xlii and xliii, shown to be one by the poetic structure and the refrain).

That the collection was not made at one time is shown by the following considerations:

(*a*) lxxii. 20 apparently once closed a collection of Davidic psalms, and its statement that the prayers of David are ended accords ill with the fact that several Davidic psalms follow, of which many are prayers, and lxxxvi is specifically called a prayer;

(b) several psalms are duplicated (xiv = liii; xl. 14–18 = lxx; cviii = lvii. 8–12 and lx. 7–14);

(c) on comparing xiv and liii, we find that Elohim (= God) stands four times in liii for Jehovah (E.V. the LORD) in xiv, and similarly lxx substitutes Elohim thrice, but retains Jehovah twice;

(d) in i–xli Jehovah stands 272 times, while Elohim stands absolutely (i.e., other than in such expressions as *my God, our God*) 15 times, whereas in xlii–lxxxiii Elohim stands 200 times and Jehovah but 40 times.

It therefore appears that there was a Jehovistic Psalter and an Elohistic Psalter, distinguished by their preference for these divine names, and that while Book I was Jehovistic, most of Books II and III formed an Elohistic Psalter. A Jehovistic appendix, lxxxiv–lxxxix, was added to the Elohistic Psalter, and Books IV and V are Jehovistic. Many scholars think the headings of the psalms indicate collections from which the psalms were taken, but these will be considered below.

It is probable that Book I is the earliest of the three main collections that make up our present Psalter. Yet this is unlikely to have been made in pre-exilic days. For Ps. xviii is duplicated in the appendix to 2 Samuel (2 Sam. xxii). If a whole collection of psalms ascribed to David already existed in Book I of the Psalter, it is hard to see why this one should be extracted for preservation in 2 Samuel, and hence its insertion there was probably earlier than the compilation of this collection. Yet that insertion could not have been made until post-exilic times. Hence we should probably date the compilation of Book I in the post-exilic period. The Elohistic Psalter followed, and Books IV and V are probably to be dated later still.

Precise dates cannot be given, but it is probable that the whole was completed before 100 B.C. The substantial agreement of the Greek text with the Hebrew would point to this conclusion, and also the fact that the Psalms of Solomon (*circa* 50 B.C.), did not secure admission suggests that the collection was already closed. Gunkel, indeed, argues that the Psalter was completed before 200 B.C.

This, however, leaves the dates of the individual psalms quite undetermined. Pfeiffer believes that most of them were written between 400 B.C. and 100 B.C., during the period when they were being assembled. At the beginning of the century Briggs assigned the majority of them to the Persian period, and especially to the time of Ezra and Nehemiah, while Duhm ascribed nearly all to the Maccabaean period, or even later. Against these views it should be noted that if the present collections come from different dates, and if they rest on earlier collections, then we are certainly carried back far for the yet earlier materials of the first collection. Moreover, it is possible that even the later collections may preserve very early materials, just as we have found very ancient fragments preserved in other books of the Old Testament.

We should be cautious of letting the pendulum swing too far in the other direction, however. Much of the present disposition to find large pre-exilic elements in the Psalter is connected with efforts to read them in terms of primitive or foreign ideas and practices. Gressmann and Widengren have read them in terms of the Babylonian psalms, and Engnell in terms of the divine kingship associated with the fertility cult that stands under such severe condemnation in the Old Testament. That Hebrew psalmody arose out of a wider background of Oriental psalmody can scarcely be denied, and there are undoubted links of form and phraseology with Babylonian and Ras Shamra texts. It is more doubtful, however, if the character and purpose of the Hebrew psalms can be established from these.

Mowinckel, whose stimulating brilliance is generally recognized, has read many of the psalms in a background of primitive magic, and has argued that all the references to "workers of iniquity" are to supposed enemies who were believed to have put a spell on a man, and that the psalms were prayers to God to break the spell. Further, he has interpreted a number of psalms in terms of the Babylonian New Year festival, and has argued that there was a comparable festival in Israel, when the Ark was carried in sacred procession, and Jehovah re-ascended his throne and the king was re-established as his vicegerent. These views have been vigorously contested by other authors. That magical ideas often prevailed in Israel is certain from the denunciations that stand in the Old Testament, and that the ideas and practices associated with the New Year festival prevailed in Israel through long periods is probable enough, and is, indeed, made more likely by the discovery of the Ras Shamra texts since Mowinckel advanced his views. Yet it is very doubtful if the post-exilic circles that collected the Psalter would have been interested in preserving texts associated with all that they so firmly rejected.

That sacred poetry was written from an early age is proved by the Song of Deborah (Judges v). Moreover, it is right to read the psalms in the background of ancient Oriental poetry, though not necessarily in terms of it, and both Babylonian and Ras Shamra texts show that sacred poetry was written from early times. That it continued to be written to a late age is proved by the Psalms of Solomon. It seems gratuitous to assume that most of what has come down to us is pre-exilic, and that there was a long hiatus to the middle of the first century B.C., when psalms of precisely similar kind to the ancient psalms preserved in the Psalter were again written. It is equally gratuitous to assume that only late psalms have come down to us, though the presumption is that a larger proportion of the earlier psalms have perished. While recognizing that psalms were probably written in Maccabaean days, the present writer doubts whether they would have been early enough to secure admission to the sources of our Psalter, though it is possible that the final editor may have incorporated a few. On the other hand, many of the individual psalms in the collections that were drawn on were probably early, and this is especially true of those in the collections used by the compiler of Book I. It should be added that Pss. i and ii probably do not really belong to Book I, but were subsequently added as an introduction to the whole Psalter.

Much discussion has centred in the subject of the "I" of the Psalms. It has been argued that it should be understood collectively, and not individually, and that the psalms where it occurs are to be understood as national psalms. Against this Balla held that they are to be understood individually. To this discussion Wheeler Robinson has contributed the fruitful suggestion that a fluid interpretation may be given in terms of the concept of corporate personality. The psalmist can identify himself with the community to which he belongs, or can pass from the collective experience to his individual experience, in which it is focused or represented. There are thus genuinely individual elements and collective elements, and cases where the two are fused.

The two modern writers who have contributed most notably to the study of the Psalter are Mowinckel and Gunkel. Some of Mowinckel's views have been noted above, and others will be referred to below. Fundamentally, Mowinckel regards the psalms as cultic poems, i.e., poems written for ritual use and employed in the cultus to accompany ritual acts. While it cannot be established that the psalms were written for cultic use, and some of them may have arisen out of individual or national experience, and while it is to be doubted if they were related to primitive magic and fertility cult usage, it is probable that Mowinckel has pointed us to a sound indication of their use. We know that in the Chronicler's day there were Temple guilds of singers, and sacred music had an important place in the ritual. Moreover, the interpretation of the Psalter in terms of Canaanite and Babylonian poems may be right to this extent, that just as those poems were recited to accompany the ritual act, being essential to the due performance of the rite and serving to interpret its significance, so the singing of the psalms may have accompanied definite ritual acts, particular psalms belonging to particular rites, and serving to interpret their significance and to lift the worshipper into their spirit, so that in a real sense the ritual act might become the organ of his spirit. But the present writer would link their cultic use, in the post-exilic age when they were collected for such use, with the religion of Judaism rather than with ancient and primitive ideas.

Nor can we be sure that all the psalms were given a cultic use, or that they were used only in the Temple ritual. Gunkel studied the types (*Gattungen*) of the psalms, and the uses they may have served. He argued that songs of thanksgiving are older than psalms of lament, and that in both cases national psalms are older than individual. The simpler the character of a psalm, and the more readily it went into one of these four primary classes, the earlier he placed it. How far we can press these presumptions is doubtful, though there can be no doubt of the stimulating quality of Gunkel's work. He denied that all the Psalms were written for Temple use, and maintained that many of them no longer presuppose cultic use, and held that many of the psalms, and especially those of individual lament, were used by the people in their own homes.

On the headings of the psalms there has been great variety of opinion. Altogether 73 psalms are ascribed to David. Whether or not this was originally intended to attribute authorship to him, it was early understood in that sense, as we see from the expanded headings to many of them. In the Greek version 12 others are ascribed to David. That David did not actually write all that are attributed to him is certain, if only because several of them presuppose the existence of the Temple (v, xxvii, xxviii, lxiii, lxviii, lxix, ci, cxxxviii). We find 55 psalms ascribed to the Director (R.V. Chief Musician), and of these some are also ascribed to David. The similarity of the form of the ascription is disguised by rendering the one "For the Chief Musician," and the other "Of David." There are 12 psalms ascribed to Asaph, 11 to the sons of Korah, one each to Moses, Solomon, Heman, Ethan and Ani, and two to Jeduthun. We find the term *mizmōr* (= psalm) at the head of 57 psalms, *maskīl* at the head of 13, *miktām* at the head of 7, while 15 psalms are called Songs of Ascents, and 18 are Hallelujah psalms, though not so described in their headings. Altogether 50 psalms have no personal ascription in their heading, while 34 have no heading at all, and are known as "orphans." Several psalms have additional notes, which are commonly held to indicate the musical accompaniment they should have, or the tune to which they should be sung (e.g., iv, v, vi, xii, xxii, xlvi, liv–lx).

A common view has been that the personal names, such as David, the Director, and terms like *mizmōr*, *maskīl*, and *miktām*, indicate the separate collections from which the compilers have drawn, and that, where more than one of these is found in a heading, it indicates that the psalm in question stood in more than one collection. The difficulty here is that it is improbable that there was, say, a Mosaic collection, containing but a single psalm. For if such a collection had contained more than one, it would be incredible for the compiler to content himself with but one. Kennett held that all the headings were of musical significance, and indicated the accompaniment in the liturgy, while Begrich has given ethnic significance to a large number of them, connecting some with Gittites (vii, lxxxi, lxxxiv), or with the Elamites (xlvi), or with the Greeks (lvi), or with the Canaanite Shimronites (vi, xii). This is more ingenious than convincing. To Mowinckel all the headings are of cultic significance, indicating the particular ritual use to which a psalm was to be put, while Engnell claims that the heading "To David" should be rendered "For the king," and indicates that the psalms concerned were used in connexion with the rites associated with the divine kingship.

The headings of the psalms are therefore still an unsolved puzzle. Of more value is it to study the ideas of the psalms. It is probable that they were written to express spiritual experience, and were used to minister to such experience, and their suitability for this purpose is evidenced by their ability to do this to the present day. Whatever similarities of form they may have to the psalms of other literatures, there is a unique quality about them which gives them enduring worth. That they express many feelings we should regard it as unworthy to share is manifestly true. Yet they contain more which expresses an exalted idea of God, and a sense of His beneficent character, where, as Sellin puts it, "a consciousness of salvation is attained which already bears an almost New Testament character."

CHAPTER XVI

THE HEBREW WISDOM LITERATURE

CERTAIN books of the Old Testament belong to what is called the Hebrew Wisdom Literature. These are Proverbs, Job, the Song of Songs, and Ecclesiastes, though it is questionable if the Song of Songs should be included amongst them. A number of psalms are akin to this literature, and beyond the limits of the Old Testament we find other cognate works. The books of Ecclesiasticus and Wisdom are obvious instances, and part of the book of Baruch (iii. 9–iv. 4) and 4 Maccabees should also be included. There are Wisdom elements in the Sayings of the Jewish Fathers (Pirqe Aboth), and in some other works.

If we think of the writers as the philosophers of the Hebrews, we may delude ourselves into thinking of them in terms of Greek philosophy. Unlike the Greeks, the Hebrews were not a speculative people. Abstract ideas have little place in their speech, for they were a fundamentally practical people. In so far as they did indulge in speculation, it was less on the ultimate nature of reality than on the nature of wisdom, less on the nature of God's Being than on the forms of His self-manifestation, less on the ultimate destiny of man than on the nature of the good life. Moreover, despite a certain element of worldly wisdom which it contained, Hebrew speculation had always a clearly religious quality.

This literature may be divided into two classes, represented by Proverbs and Job. The one embodied a shrewd practical philosophy of life, while the other grapples with one of the major problems of life. Yet even here, as will appear below, the interest is more practical than abstract, more religious than intellectual. The nearest approach to abstract speculation in the Old Testament is found in the first section of the book of

Proverbs, and especially in its climax in chapter viii, where Wisdom is hypostatized.

Proverbial sayings, embodying keen observation often picturesquely expressed, must be very ancient in Israel, as amongst other peoples. In the Old Testament we find a number of these preserved (e.g., 1 Kings xx. 11, Jer. xxxi. 29), and in the book of Proverbs we find many literary expansions of older and briefer observations. Such sayings could easily cross frontiers, and there is an international character about this kind of wisdom. Indeed, there is some evidence that part of the book of Proverbs rests on an Egyptian written source. But in its oral stage wisdom could easily travel, and there are references in the Old Testament to peoples famed for their wisdom, e.g., Edom (Jer. xlix. 7, Obad. 8, Job ii. 11), Tyre (Ezek. xxviii. 2–7), Egypt (Gen. xli. 8, Exod. vii. 11, 1 Kings iv. 30, Isa. xix. 11), and Babylon (Isa. xliv. 25, Jer. l. 35, li. 57).

There are passages in the Old Testament where wise men are mentioned alongside priests and prophets as a recognized channel of instruction (Jer. xviii. 18; cf. viii. 8, Ezek. vii. 26), and the wise men seem to have had their pupils as well as the prophets (Prov. ii. 1, iii. 1, iv. 1, 10, v. 1, 13, xxii. 17–21). They cannot be thought of merely as custodians of proverbial sayings, but rather as instructors of youth in the art of living. We find in them none ot the missionary purpose of Deutero-Isaiah or of the author of Jonah, none of the burning passion to fight against injustice and evil that marked the prophets, but rather a desire to live a decent, comfortable and happy life, observing healthy moral standards, and playing the part of good citizens. Yet they recognized that only a religious basis for life could produce this. The fear of the Lord was for them the beginning of Wisdom (Prov. i. 7, ix. 10, Ps. cxi. 10, Job xxviii. 28), and obedience to His will the only way to worthy living.

All who followed their guidance showed true wisdom, while those who rejected it were fools. The fools figure prominently in the book of Proverbs, and it is clear that the wise thought there were many of them, and of many kinds. There are passages which suggest that the wise were not prepared to waste much time on the fools, who were unlikely to respond (Prov. xvi. 22, xxvii. 22). Amongst the fools the slothful have a prominent place, for the wise had a salutary recognition of the value of discipline and work. They set a high standard of sexual morality before their disciples, and continually warned them against the lures of the "strange woman."

Of a profounder character altogether is the book of Job, wrestling with the practical aspects of the problem of innocent suffering, and seeking to give a religious message to those who were tortured with the experience. It is often claimed that a parallel to this book can be found in what is called the Babylonian Job, but there is found there nothing to compare with the spiritual penetration of this book. The Babylonian sufferer reflects on the inscrutable ways of the gods, and laments that sacrifice and prayer are unavailing to deliver him from his misery and misfortune, until Marduk rewards him by delivering him and he utters his cry of thanksgiving. Neither this, nor another Babylonian text in which a miserable sufferer is converted by a pious preacher to resign himself humbly to the will of God, can approach the insight and the message of the book of Job. The resemblances are but superficial, while the differences are profound.

Much shallower is the pessimism of the philosophy of the writer of Ecclesiastes, who is impressed with the futility of life. Here, more than anywhere else in the Old Testament, Greek influence has been claimed, and while the direct influence of any Greek school can but doubtfully be sustained, it is possible that Greek ideas had been mediated to the author in various ways. From whatever source he received his ideas, they produced in him a more negative philosophy than marked the rest of the Wise.

Speaking generally, the Wisdom writings that have come down to us lack form and system, apart from the book of Job. They consist mainly of casual observations, rather than an integrated system of thought and teaching. It may be added that while the beginnings of Wisdom must be placed far back in the past, the Wisdom books that have come down to us are all of post-exilic origin in their present form.

CHAPTER XVII

THE BOOK OF PROVERBS

T H E Hebrew word *māshāl*, which we render by *proverb*, is much wider in meaning than our word. It is the name given to the Balaam *oracles*; in Isa. xiv. 4, it is applied to the *taunt song* against the king of Babylon; it is sometimes applied to *parables*, or *allegories*. It is also used for a *pithy saying*, in the sense of our word.

It should not surprise us, therefore, to find that the book of Proverbs is not just a collection of pithy sayings, though it contains many such. It is a collection of varied character. It is ascribed in its title to Solomon, and again in x. 1 he is said to be the author of the collection that follows, and in xxv. 1 he is again named as the ultimate author of a collection which the men of Hezekiah copied. The ascription of this and other Wisdom writings to Solomon is in accordance with the Hebrew way of "telescoping," as McFadyen calls it. All the Law is ascribed to Moses, all the Conquest to Joshua, most of the sacred lyric poetry to David, and all the Wisdom literature to Solomon. That Solomon was not the author of our book as it stands is clear. For apart from the reference to the men of Hezekiah, we find the attribution of some sayings to "the wise men" (xxiv. 23), of some to Agur (xxx. 1), and of some to Lemuel (xxxi. 1). The book manifestly consists of several separate collections, which may best be considered separately.

(*a*) The first section (i. 1–ix. 18, of which the first six verses are an introduction to the whole book) is different from all the others in the integration of its material into a series of short essays. It is also notable for its hypostatization of wisdom, chiefly in chap. viii, but also in i. 20–23, ix. 1–6, and, by implication, in iv. 5–9. It is probably the latest section of the book, and its date may be as late as the middle of the third century B.C.

(*b*) The second section (x. 1–xxii. 16), is the oldest in the book. Normally each verse is a self-contained couplet, independent of its neighbours. In several cases we find a duplicated line, but with a different parallel line (e.g., x. 15 and xviii. 11; xv. 33 and xviii. 12; xix. 12 and xx. 2). It is possible that sayings from a pre-literary stage have been differently filled out in the literary stage. What we have in this collection is a series of literary proverbs, save that a few single-line sayings have been preserved. This collection may be of pre-exilic origin, though this is disputed by Pfeiffer. The evidence for this view is not strong, though it satisfies Gressmann, Sellin and Oesterley. It rests in part on the consideration that we have pre-exilic evidence for the existence of a class of the wise, whose sayings are as likely to have been preserved as the prophetic oracles.

(*c*) The third section (xxii. 17–xxiv. 34), is subdivided by Oesterley into three (xxii. 17–xxiii. 14; xxiii. 15–xxiv. 22; xxiv. 23–34), though he holds the last two to be closely connected with the first. The reason for the separation of the first of these sections is its connexion with the Egyptian text, *The Wisdom of Amen-em-ope*, while the reason for the separation of the third is its new heading. The Egyptian text dates from the eighth or seventh century B.C., and is believed to have been used directly by the author of the Hebrew passage, though his work is not a mere translation of the other. Much significance is attached to the fact that the word rendered "excellent things" in Prov. xxii. 20, had always provided a difficulty until the publication of the Egyptian text. Its only known meaning elsewhere in Hebrew is "three days ago." It is almost identical with the Hebrew word for "thirty," however, and in the Egyptian text we read: "Consider these thirty chapters." Gressmann has argued that this little Hebrew collection contained thirty sayings, and to-day it is agreed by most that in Prov. xxii. 20 we should read "thirty sayings" for the unintelligible word. The dependence of the Hebrew writer did not cause him to forfeit his independence of outlook. The date of this section can scarcely be earlier than the seventh century B.C., and may be a good deal later.

(*d*) The fourth section (xxv–xxix) is believed by Sellin,

Oesterley and Gemser to be reliably attributed to the period
of Hezekiah. On internal grounds this collection is pronounced
later than x. 1–xxii. 16, but all these scholars find evidences of
the pre-exilic period. It should be noted, however, that they
rely in part on the references to the king as evidence that the
Hebrew monarchy was still in existence. Against this Gray
noted that in Ecclus. vii. 5 we read: "Display not thy wisdom
before the king," in a passage dating from *circa* 180 B.C.,
and argued that by a careful comparison of all the references
to the king in Proverbs and in Ecclesiastes and Ecclesiasticus,
it may be demonstrated that none of them demand a pre-
exilic date.

(*e*) The fifth section (xxx. 1–14) is brief, and contains
sayings of the unknown Agur. Some editors believe his share
does not extend beyond verse 6.

(*f*) The sixth section (xxx. 15–33) is an excerpt from an
unknown source.

(*g*) The seventh section (xxxi. 1–9) preserves the sayings
of Lemuel, of whom again we know nothing.

(*h*) The final section (xxxi. 10–31), is an alphabetic acrostic
poem in praise of the virtuous woman, which stands quite by
itself in character, and whose language marks it as post-exilic.
It should be added that in the Greek version these last four
sections stand in a relatively different order. This may indicate
that they were added after the compilation of the book of
Proverbs as a whole.

Unless we suppose that the book grew by successive
stages—a view which is improbable in view of the relative
ages of the various parts, and especially in view of the fact
that the latest section stands first—we must place the compilation of the book after the latest of the main sources on
which it drew. Here, therefore, as so frequently elsewhere, we
find a late collection, embodying some genuinely ancient
material.

CHAPTER XVIII

THE BOOK OF JOB

T H E book of Job is the greatest work of genius in the Old Testament, and one of the world's artistic masterpieces. It consists of:

(*a*) chaps. i f., forming a prose Prologue, telling of Job's piety and the Satan's cynicism, and the divine permission to test Job;

(*b*) chaps. iii–xxxi, containing a dialogue in poetry between Job and his friends in three cycles, the third of which is incomplete;

(*c*) chaps. xxxii–xxxvii, containing the speeches of Elihu, a new character who appears and makes his speeches in succession, without interruption, and then disappears from the scene;

(*d*) chaps. xxxviii–xli, containing two Divine speeches, separated only by two verses from Job;

(*e*) chap. xlii. 2–6, recording Job's submission;

(*f*) chap. xlii. 7–17, containing a prose Epilogue, recording Job's restoration.

Certain parts of the book are quite certainly not original, and others are probably secondary. Here we may note (*a*) the Elihu speeches (xxxii–xxxvii), (*b*) the second Divine speech (xl. 6–xli. 34), and (*c*) the Wisdom chapter (xxviii).

The Elihu speeches can be dropped from the book without affecting its structure, whereas they presuppose the rest of the book. No notice is taken of Elihu in the Divine speeches, and in the Epilogue judgment is pronounced on Job and his friends, but again Elihu is ignored. Cornill and Budde defend these speeches on the ground that only here is a solution to the problem of suffering offered. But the solution is that the purpose of suffering is to purge the heart of pride, and that this is Job's sin. That this is not the author's solution is clear

143

from the Prologue, where he says that the purpose of Job's suffering is to vindicate God's trust in him.

The second Divine speech consists of lengthy descriptions of Behemoth and Leviathan, which stand either for the hippopotamus and the crocodile, or are mythical creatures. These descriptions contrast with the swift and brilliant descriptions of the first speech. Moreover, if this second speech followed Job's submission, it comes, as Peake observes, perilously near nagging. Some writers have rejected both Divine speeches, but this would leave the dialogue in the air, and no sufficient grounds can be produced for the excision of the first speech. It is said that it is inconsistent with the Epilogue, where Job is pronounced in the right, while here he is rebuked. But there he is pronounced in the right in relation to the Satan's charge, i.e., right in his maintenance that he was not suffering for his sins, whereas here he is rebuked for making wild charges against God in his ignorance of all the facts. Only omniscience could justify his charges, and omniscience belongs only to God. Hence, we should retain the first speech, while the loss of the second is rather a gain.

The Wisdom chapter is a great poem, akin to the first section of the book of Proverbs, but out of place on the lips of Job or of his friends. If Job had already reached such a view, there would have been no need for the Divine speech, since he would already have perceived what it declared.

Many writers hold that the Prologue and the Epilogue come from a different hand from the rest of the book. They believe they are older and were taken over by the author who composed the dialogue, who did not feel himself free to discard the Epilogue, though they regard it as a blemish on the work. Dhorme and Hölscher, rightly in the present writer's view, reject this theory. The author probably worked with a traditional story of a righteous sufferer, but created his whole work himself.

It is probable that there has been some loss from the dialogue. Its plan is as follows: after an introductory soliloquy by Job, the three friends speak in turn, being each answered by Job; there follows a second cycle, and then a third, but incomplete, cycle; a closing soliloquy of Job's appeals to God to vindicate him, and is followed by the Divine speech. By some it has been thought that the incomplete third cycle is intended to indicate that the friends had run out of arguments, but there is matter that does not seem to fit the lips on which it is placed, and hence many believe the third cycle was once complete, but is now disordered and mutilated. Baumgärtel holds, on the other hand, that originally there was only a single cycle of speeches, iv–xiii, followed by a soliloquy of Job's, now distributed in chaps. xvi, xix, xxiii and xxxi. This seems to be unnecessarily radical. Again, Lindblom has recently advanced what appears to be an unduly complicated theory of the growth of the book. He not only finds the Prologue and Epilogue to be older than the dialogue, but regards them as composite. He believes an Israelite writer introduced the Satan and Job's wife into an originally Edomite work, and substituted a new ending, to which a further ending, based on the old Edomite one, was later added. For the rest Lindblom follows the view above outlined, save that he rejects as worthless xlii. 1–6 along with the second Divine speech. It would seem better to retain this, which would follow on xl. 4 f. with the omission of the second Divine speech, and which would provide a fitting climax to the book.

Mention should be made of the view of Stevenson, that the poetic portion of the book is quite independent of the Prologue and Epilogue. He therefore studies this by itself and holds that Job's sufferings are not due to disease but to persecution. The friends then become the heroes of the book, giving sound advice in which the message of the book is to be found, while Job becomes a rebel against God, whose rebellion is finally overcome. It is hard to think that the poetical part of the book ever circulated by itself, without any setting or explanation of what it was about.

Accepting then the Prologue, Job's soliloquy, and three cycles of dialogue, Job's closing soliloquy, the first Divine speech, Job's submission, and the Epilogue, we may find the message of the book to be an integrated whole. The problem it deals with is innocent suffering. It is sometimes said that prior to the book of Job the Hebrew view was that there was no such thing as innocent suffering. This is not correct. Abel is not represented as being murdered because he deserved to be, and the prophets were continually denouncing the injustice of the sufferings of the downtrodden. Deuteronomy had taught that the nation always reaped the fruits of its sins or its righteousness, and with the emphasis on the individual laid by Jeremiah and Ezekiel, it would appear that in certain circles there had developed the rigid view that desert and fortune were invariably matched. These circles are represented by Job's friends, and against this view the book is directed.

The writer wishes to insist, first of all, that there is such a thing as innocent suffering. Hence it is declared unequivocally in the Prologue that Job is suffering innocently. The reason for his suffering is given to the reader, since it was necessary to give it to establish that Job was suffering innocently. But it was concealed from Job throughout, since otherwise the book would have brought no message to men who must suffer in the dark. Job is suffering to vindicate God's trust in him, and in his suffering he is thus unwittingly serving God.

The dialogue offers no solution to the mystery of suffering. Neither Job nor his friends could deduce the reason. Hence the intellectual problem is unsolved. Yet the author would express his faith that there is a reason, hidden in the heart of God, as the reason for Job's suffering was, and that it is futile to try to fathom it. The purport of the Divine speech is that the margins of man's ignorance are so great that he should not presume to judge, and Job is rebuked for his presumption in passing judgment on God.

This intellectual agnosticism, however, is but the basis for a religious message. If there is such a thing as innocent suffering, then suffering is not necessarily the proof that a man is abandoned by God, and if the sufferer will have faith in God and be humbly submissive to Him, then he may enjoy the fellowship of God even in his suffering. It is true that in the Epilogue Job is delivered from his suffering and his fortunes restored. But the Epilogue belongs to the form of the book, and not to its message. The suffering was the form Job's trial took, and when the verdict of acquittal was passed, it would have been intolerable for the trial to go on. Nowhere in the dialogue does Job regret his integrity, or break down on the issue on which he is being tested.

If, then, the Epilogue is of the artistry of the book, Job's final word must be the climax of its message. And it is something deeper than the issue of the Babylonian Job, to which reference has been made in a previous chapter. Not deliverance from his suffering, but peace in his suffering, may be the portion of the innocent sufferer. "I had heard of thee by the hearing of the ear; but now mine eye seeth thee. Wherefore I abhor myself, and repent in dust and ashes," cries Job (xlii. 5 f.). Here he declares that the knowledge of God that had come to him in his suffering was as superior to anything he had before known as the knowledge of sight is to the knowledge of a rumour. This is to declare that even suffering may be an enrichment if in his suffering the sufferer has fellowship with God. Nowhere is there a clearer illustration of the fact that Hebrew wisdom is practical rather than speculative, and religious rather than intellectual.

That the book comes from the post-exilic age is certain, if it is rightly held to have a perversion of the teaching of Jeremiah and Ezekiel as its background. Its precise age cannot be determined, but it is probable that it should be dated in the fifth century B.C. Some writers have contended for an earlier date, including Pfeiffer, who would place it in the time of Jeremiah, while some have argued for a later date, including Eissfeldt, Steuernagel, and Volz, who would place it in the fourth century B.C., and Cornill, who placed it in the third century B.C. So late a date would hardly leave time for the various additions to be made to the book before the Greek version was made.

CHAPTER XIX

THE FIVE ROLLS

T H E five books Song of Songs, Ruth, Lamentations, Ecclesiastes and Esther, which stand together in the Hebrew Canon, are known as the Five Rolls, or Megilloth. They were each read publicly at one of the annual festivals, though how ancient this practice was cannot be determined.

(a) Song of Songs

In its title this book is ascribed to Solomon, but on linguistic grounds alone this can be rejected. Some would attribute it to the pre-exilic period, though most assign it to post-exilic days, perhaps somewhere about 400 B.C., or even later. It contains at least one Persian loan-word, and perhaps a Greek loan-word, and neither of these is likely to date from a pre-exilic time. The mention of Tirzah (vi. 4) as parallel to Jerusalem is thought by some to favour an early date, but against this it is suggested that a writer from a time after the Samaritan feud might prefer to use the name of the older northern capital. The book is notable for the great beauty of its style, and for its highly poetic, if somewhat bold, metaphors. Attention is centred in its interpretation, on which the greatest variety of view has prevailed.

Traditionally the Jews have interpreted it as an allegory of the history of Israel, while this view was re-adapted in the Christian Church to yield an allegory of Christ's dealings with His Church. The greatest extravagances of exegesis have been indulged in, such as Hengstenberg's interpretation of the Shulammite's navel (vii. 3) as the chalice from which the Church revives those thirsting for salvation, and Wordsworth's conclusion from the relative number of the concubines and the queens (v. 8), that the sectarians should outnumber the true Church. On such principles anything may mean anything.

The abandonment of this view led to the view that we have a dialogue or drama. This has taken several forms. To one school there were two characters, Solomon and the Shulammite, whom the king wooed and won. To Ewald, who had much following in the latter half of the nineteenth century, it was a three-character drama, presenting the story of the triumph of love over the blandishments of a king. Here the Shulammite remained faithful to her rustic swain, and resisted the king's advances, until he allowed her to return to her lover. By some the drama is further fitted with a chorus.

At the turn of the century, the view that we have a cycle of wedding songs held the field. This was based on Wetzstein's study of modern Syrian customs, and those who adopted it held that in ancient Palestine the bride and the bridegroom were crowned and treated as king and queen during the seven days of the celebration. Poems, to-day called *wasfs*, were sung in their honour, and the bride had to do a sword dance. It was held that we have in the Song a selection of the cycle current in a single locality. Against this view it is urged that we cannot safely argue from modern Syria to ancient Palestine.

The last quarter of a century has seen a new view gain currency, according to which we have here an ancient liturgy of the Adonis cult. This view was propounded by Meek, who has had some followers. On this view the Song belonged to the old fertility cult, the Shulammite representing the goddess in the sacred marriage with the king, whereby the springs of fertility were released. It is hard to think that a liturgy of the condemned cult would have been brought into the sacred literature of Judaism, but it is claimed that the Song was reinterpreted when it was absorbed into Judaism. It might have been supposed that it would have been given the plain marks of that into which it was absorbed, whereas only the marks of that from which it was taken are found by this school.

That there are references to Adonis rites in the Song is probably true, but that it was a cult poem is very doubtful. It is known that in the first century A.D. there were some who regarded these poems as ordinary love songs, and it is probably best to give them this, their most natural, interpretation. To the writer it seems probable that they come

from a single author, and that there is a conscious arrangement, and there are some references to the Adonis rites. Yet
fundamentally the songs express pure human love, and the
mutual loyalty of the marriage relation, though with a bold-
ness we should not emulate. At the end of the first century
A.D. it was still disputed whether this book should be accepted
into the Canon.

(b) Ruth

The book of Ruth relates a story that is laid in the age of
the Judges, and on that account it was transferred in the
Greek version to follow the book of Judges. It tells of Ruth's
entry into Israel with her widowed mother-in-law, and her
subsequent marriage with Boaz, who was a kinsman of her
late husband's.

That the author has worked with old and reliable traditions is very probable, but that the book comes from the post-
exilic period is almost certain. This is supported by the following considerations:

(a) the opening verse suggests that the author was familiar
with the Deuteronomic edition of the book of Judges;

(b) the explanation of the custom described in iv. 7 implies
that it was now obsolete;

(c) the language and style have some late features, though
in many respects they are based on good early models.

The marriage of Ruth with Boaz is akin to levirate marriage, though the relationship is more distant. In Deut. xxv.
9 it is provided that when a brother-in-law declines the duty
of levirate marriage, the wronged woman shall draw off his
shoe and publicly spit in his face. In Ruth iv. 9, Ruth is not
present, and there is no spitting, while the drawing off of
the shoe is interpreted as a mere commercial sign. It is possible
that we have here a modification of the practice of Deut. xxv.
9 coming from a later age, but more probable that the more
distant relationship of the kinsman offers the explanation. As
the next of kin he was entitled to the first refusal of the pro-
perty and of Ruth's hand, but there was less stigma upon him
for his refusal in view of his more distant relationship.

By many scholars the book is ascribed to the period of

Nehemiah and Ezra, and interpreted as a political tract, protesting against their opposition to mixed marriages by its reminder that David had Moabite blood in his veins. The book does not read like a political tract, and if it were it might be very differently interpreted. Nehemiah and Ezra were opposed to mixed marriages because of the religious laxity they led to. But in its most exclusive moments, Judaism was not averse to the receiving of proselytes. When Ruth enters Israel, before her marriage with Boaz, she renounces her own race and religion, and embraces her mother-in-law's. She is therefore represented as a proselyte. Hence to anyone who cited the case of David's ancestress against Nehemiah and Ezra, this book offered the retort that Ruth was no longer an alien, but a proselyte, at the time of her marriage to Boaz. Nevertheless, it is very doubtful if it was written for a polemic purpose at all, though the fifth century date may well be correct.

(c) Lamentations

The book of Lamentations consists of five poems, of which the first four are alphabetic acrostics, and the fifth, though not an acrostic, contains the same number of verses as the letters of the Hebrew alphabet. The rhythm of the first four is 3 : 2, and this has given the name Qinah (= elegy) to this metre; the rhythm of the fifth is 3 : 3.

The traditional ascription of the book to Jeremiah led to its transfer to follow Jeremiah in the Greek version. This ascription may be due to 2 Chron. xxxv. 25, which states that Jeremiah composed a dirge on the death of Josiah. That it is to be rejected is established by the following considerations:

(a) the statement in ii. 9 that Judah's prophets find no vision from the Lord suggests that the writer was not one of them;

(b) the expectation of imminent trouble for the Chaldaeans (iii. 64–66), does not seem to have been shared by Jeremiah;

(c) the writer's hope that Egypt would have sent help (iv. 7), contrasts with Jeremiah's consistent protest against reliance upon Egypt;

(d) if, as some believe, iv. 20 refers to Zedekiah, its laudatory view is different from Jeremiah's;

(*e*) the view of v. 7 is one against which Jeremiah had directly protested (Jer. xxxi. 29 f.);

(*f*) considerations of language and style are against Jeremianic authorship.

There are reasons for thinking that not all the poems are from one hand. These include the following:

(*a*) the order of the letters of the alphabet in chaps. ii–iv differs from that in chap. i, and the abnormal order is found elsewhere in the Old Testament, showing that at one time it was regarded as the correct order;

(*b*) Thenius noted that chaps. ii and iv are distinguished by a style superior to that of the other chapters, being characterized by the greatest wealth of thought and the most finished form;

(*c*) Gray noted that in chaps. i, ii and iv the alphabetic sections correspond to the divisions of thought, and yield true strophes, whereas in chap. iii this is not so;

(*d*) Gray further noted differences of technique in the use of parallelism, whereby chaps. i and iii may be distinguished from ii and iv, while ii may also be distinguished from iv.

The poems all lament the fall of Jerusalem, and while chap. iii may perhaps be post-exilic, the others almost certainly come from a time shortly after the fall of the city, and it is commonly believed that ii and iv may come from the hand of a single eye-witness. Cornill and Sellin think the author of chap. iii, which is the poorest of the book, may have had Jeremiah in mind. The compilation of the book must be placed in the post-exilic age, but there is no reason to come down far below the period of the Return.

(*d*) *Ecclesiastes*

Ecclesiastes is a book of the Wisdom literature, dealing with the meaninglessness of all things. It purports to have been written by a king who was the son of David, and hence has been traditionally ascribed to Solomon. The reasons for the rejection of this tradition are:

(*a*) the author implies that many generations of Israelites had preceded him in Jerusalem (i. 16, ii. 9), whereas in Solomon's days but one could be claimed;

(b) the author frequently writes from the standpoint of a subject condemning the administration (iii. 16, iv. 1);

(c) the author seems to be living in a province of a great empire, and makes bitter observations on the system of rule, with its use of the spy (x. 20);

(d) the conditions of anarchy prevalent in the land (iv. 13–16, x. 16–20) suggest the last century of the Persian period or the Greek period;

(e) the linguistic evidence is decisively against Solomonic authorship.

While these considerations are of varying weight, their cumulative force is decisive. More disputed is the significance of those features in the book which have caused its unity to be questioned. Apart from the closing verses (xii. 9–14), which almost all hold to be a later addition there are inner contradictions in the book (e.g., ii. 15 f. and ii. 26). Cornill, who championed the unity of the book, found in these the varying moods of a single person, while long ago Herder maintained that we have a dialogue between two persons. Others have followed McNeile in holding a theory of two glossators, while Siegfried thought he could detect no less than eight hands in the book. Of McNeile's glossators, the one was believed to have added maxims of worldly wisdom (called the *Hokmah* glossator), and the other the orthodox observations (called the *Hasid* glossator), which are believed to have enabled the book to secure admission to the sacred collection. Examples of the *Hokmah* glossator's work are found in iv. 5, vii. 1, 7, viii. 1, and of the *Hasid* glossator's in ii. 26, vii. 18b. Galling has offered a fresh defence of the unity of the book's authorship on the view that the writer often quoted a current maxim in order to add his own comment, exposing its hollowness.

The question of the possible dependence of the book on foreign thought has been actively discussed in the last two decades. Langdon held that it reflected Babylonian influence, and Humbert Egyptian, but far more canvassed has been a theory of dependence on Greek writers. Sellin traced the influence of Epicurean, Stoic, and Heracleitean thought, while more recent writers, including Ranston, have favoured the influence of the early Gnomic writers, Hesiod and Theognis.

Ranston collects a large number of parallels of both thought and expression, which he holds to be too striking to be accidental.

By most scholars the book is ascribed to the Greek period, somewhere in the third century B.C. If Friedländer's suggestion that the poor wise man of ix. 15 was Archimedes is correct, and the incident referred to in that passage was the siege of Syracuse, then we should be brought down to the end of the century. It should be added that Dornseiff, who places its composition between 490 B.C. and 180 B.C., has argued that it is a pseudepigraph, in the form of an address by Solomon from beyond the grave (cf. i. 12).

(e) Esther

The book of Esther has enjoyed extraordinary popularity amongst the Jews. It narrates the story of a projected pogrom of the Jews which was skilfully turned into bloody vengeance on their foes. There is no mention of God in the book, and it breathes a spirit of intense nationalism. The story is laid in the days of Ahasuerus, who is to-day normally identified with Xerxes (485–465 B.C.)

That it is fiction and not history is agreed by most. Xerxes did not have a queen named Esther, and it is unlikely that he had a Jewish queen at all. Moreover, Mordecai is represented as having been carried into captivity 112 years before the accession of Xerxes (ii. 6), which would make him improbably old at the time of the story. Hoschander has argued for a historical basis of the story by transferring it to the reign of Artaxerxes II (404–359 B.C.), but this is improbable. If this view were correct, we should have to bring the composition of the book far below this date to explain its garbled version.

Cornill found in it a reflection of the Maccabaean struggle, but this seems unlikely. It is, however, possible that it was written to express the nationalistic feelings that attached to the celebration of the Maccabaean victories, and it is significant that the feast of Purim, whose establishment the book records, was celebrated on the two days following Nicanor's day (1 Macc. vii. 49, 2 Macc. xv. 36).

For the origin of the book many writers have turned to Oriental mythology, and many have been the derivations proposed for the word Purim, which has no satisfactory Hebrew etymology. To Zimmern Mordecai was but Marduk, the god of Babylon, and *purim* but disguised *puhru*, or the assembly of the gods. To Jensen the story resolved itself into the reflection of a conflict between Babylonian and Elamite gods, Esther being Ishtar and Vashti an Elamite goddess Mashti, Mordecai being Marduk and Haman an Elamite god Humman. To Lagarde the Persian feast of Farwardigan provided the origin of Purim, and this view has recently been advocated by Lewy, while Pfeiffer holds that the book is fiction pure and simple, and that the author invented both the feast of Purim and its name, to express the popular feelings in the time of Hyrcanus, and to extend by two days the patriotic and secular celebration of Nicanor's day. To Pfeiffer the word *Purim* is as arbitrary an invention as *Kodak*.

From this welter of views no certain conclusions can be drawn, though it is doubtful if the author wrote the story entirely out of his own head. He seems to have had access to some good sources of information on things Persian, and the nucleus of his story may be older than his book. That he wrote it at some time in the second century B.C. seems on every ground probable. Mordecai and Esther are both unmentioned in the great hymn in praise of the Fathers, in Ecclus. xliv–xlix, and it is therefore probable that the book was unknown to Ben Sira *circa* 180 B.C. Yet there is no need to come down more than a few decades below 180 B.C. for the atmosphere of nationalism that would provide a ready welcome for this book.

CHAPTER XX

THE BOOK OF DANIEL

WITH the book of Daniel we come to the only fully apocalyptic book in the Old Testament. It has been observed above that there are portions of some of the prophetic books which closely approximate to apocalyptic, or which are regarded by some as fully apocalyptic, and it should be recognized that apocalyptic, while distinguishable from prophecy, is the child of prophecy and its development on one side of its message. But here we have a whole book which is normally assigned to this class of literature. There are, however, some parts of the first half of the book which would not, by themselves, be properly described as apocalyptic. In the Hebrew Canon this book stands quite separate from the prophets, and various explanations of this have been proposed. In the Greek version it was transferred to stand beside the prophets, and received some additions.

The first half of the book consists of stories told about Daniel or about his three friends, while the second half consists of visions seen by Daniel. The scene of the whole is laid in Babylon in the sixth century B.C. Part of the book is in Aramaic (ii. 4b–vii. 28), and part in Hebrew (i. 1–ii. 4a, viii–xii), but the change of language does not coincide with the change from story to vision. Moreover, in the first half of the book there is recorded a vision of Nebuchadnezzar which has many points of connexion with the first of the visions of the second half of the book.

Many considerations go to show that the stories of the work are not historical, and that we have not to do here with the creation of a sixth century prophet. Of these the following may be mentioned:

(a) the reference to the siege and capture of Jerusalem in the third year of Jehoiakim (i. 1) is unhistorical;

(b) Belshazzar was not the son of Nebuchadrezzar (v. 11), but the son of Nabonidus, of whom we are reliably told in extra-Biblical sources that he was unrelated to Nebuchadrezzar;

(c) Belshazzar was not king of Babylon (v. 1, vii. 1), though he was charged for many years with the administration of the kingdom, while his father Nabonidus, who was the last king of the Chaldaean empire, lived in Tema, in Arabia;

(d) in contemporary documents dates were accordingly never reckoned by the years of Belshazzar (vii. 1, viii. 1), as they would have been if he had been king, either solely or jointly;

(e) Darius the Mede (v. 31, vi. 28) is an unhistorical character for whom history leaves no room, since Cyrus directly annexed the kingdom when he conquered the empire of Nabonidus;

(f) the use of the word "Chaldaeans," to denote a learned priestly class is an anachronism, paralleled in classical authors, but impossible in the sixth century B.C., when the Chaldaeans, in the ethnic sense of the word, were the rulers of Babylon;

(g) it is inconsistent with all we know of the Babylonian priesthood that a Hebrew should have been admitted to be its head (ii. 48) and inconsistent with the rigid loyalty to his own religion, ascribed to Daniel, that he should have consented to serve in a heathen priesthood;

(h) the Aramaic sections are not written in seventh-century Babylonian Aramaic, but in Aramaic that can be definitely dated later than the fifth century, and with probability not earlier than the third century B.C., while the Hebrew is late and inferior to the Aramaic;

(i) the many Persian loan-words in the vocabulary of the book suggest a long period of Persian influence, while the few Greek loan-words suggest the Greek period for a background, and this is emphasized by the use of the Greek word *symphonia* as the name of a musical instrument, since that word is first found in Greek literature in this sense in the second century B.C.;

(j) the non-mention of Daniel in the hymn in praise of the Fathers in Ecclus. xliv–xlix suggests that the book was unknown to the author.

For the positive dating of the book we have the following considerations:

(a) the interest in chaps. ii and vii centres in the fourth kingdom, and in the enduring kingdom that should follow it, and it is clear that the reference in both cases is the same;

(b) the Little Horn of vii. 8, 25, is to be identified with the Little Horn of viii. 9–12, where the interpretation explicitly brings us into the Greek period;

(c) the vision of chap. ix culminates in an attack on the Jews similar to that of chaps. vii and viii;

(d) the vision of chaps. x–xii culminates in a similar attack on the Jews, to be followed by the overthrow of the oppressor, and the resurrection to everlasting glory of certain righteous ones, and to everlasting shame of certain others;

(e) that the culmination of all these visions is bound together is reinforced by the use of the phrase "abomination of desolation," in slightly varying forms in viii. 13, ix. 27, xi. 31, xii. 11, to describe the culminating offence of the oppressor;

(f) that the culmination of the last vision is to be placed in the time of Antiochus Epiphanes is made clear by the detailed history of the Greek period set forth in chap. xi down to the time of Antiochus, but not beyond;

(g) the knowledge of the Greek period, in contrast to that of the sixth century B.C. is so precise that chap. xi is recognized as a first-class historical source for the period.

It is therefore clear that the composition of the book is to be placed in the second century B.C., in the time of Antiochus Epiphanes, who proscribed the Jewish religion, forbade its practices, profaned the Temple and turned it into the seat of heathen worship, with a heathen altar and idol—presumably an image of himself, since he claimed to be Zeus incarnate— and who compelled the Jews to offer profane sacrifices until the Maccabaean revolt broke out. In 1 Macc. i. 54, the heathen altar of Antiochus is called the "abomination of desolation," and we are told that the Temple was desecrated for a period of slightly over three years, and the legitimate sacrifices interrupted for a somewhat longer period. Some of the cryptic references of the book of Daniel probably find their explanation here. We read of a half week (ix. 27), and of "a time and times and half a time" (vii. 25, xii. 7), which should probably be understood to mean three and a half years, and of two thousand three hundred evenings and mornings (viii. 14), which should probably be resolved into one thousand one hundred and fifty days.

It should be clear that it is not unwillingness to allow the

CHAPTER XXI

CHRONICLES—EZRA—NEHEMIAH

THE remaining books of the Old Testament form a single work, though in the Hebrew MSS. Chronicles follows Ezra and Nehemiah, and is not divided into two books as in modern versions, which follow the Greek. It is thought by many that Ezra and Nehemiah, which deal with a period not dealt with elsewhere in the sacred collection, were brought into the collection before Chronicles, which retraverses the story of earlier books, and especially of Samuel and Kings.

For the view that these books constitute a single work, the following considerations are relied on:

(a) the opening verses of Ezra stand also in a mutilated form at the end of 2 Chronicles;

(b) the style in the editorial parts of the books is the same;

(c) the characteristic interests of the editor are the same throughout, and include veneration for the Temple and its personnel, and a fondness for genealogies and statistics.

We are therefore carried down to the time of Ezra and Nehemiah at the earliest for the composition of the work. Ostensibly Ezra and Nehemiah were contemporaries, and both belonged to the reign of Artaxerxes. If this was Artaxerxes I, Ezra would seem to have come to Jerusalem in 458 B.C., and Nehemiah in 444 B.C. Many scholars to-day hold that Ezra belonged to the time of Artaxerxes II, and that the order of the two men has been reversed by the Chronicler. This view rests on the following considerations:

(a) whereas the work of Nehemiah was the rebuilding of the walls of Jerusalem, Ezra found them already built (Ezra ix. 9);

(b) there is a general absence of reference to the other in the memoirs of each, and on the few occasions when both names occur in a single context, there is reason to suspect the editorial hand;

possibility of accurate prophecy which dictates this conclusion, as is often alleged, but the study of evidence. The inaccuracy of knowledge of the period in which Daniel is placed, and the accuracy of knowledge of a later period, have both to be considered. The date of the book can then be defined with precision just before the death of Antiochus, which took place in 164 B.C. The stories were told to hearten people during the struggle, and the apocalyptic hopes were of the expected imminent divine intervention to sweep away earthly empires and inaugurate the age of enduring righteousness. The horizon of the prophets had been reached, and the Golden Age was at hand.

While there is widespread agreement amongst scholars on all this, there are many unsolved problems connected with the book, on which there is less agreement.

(a) While there is agreement that the book in its present form dates from the second century B.C., there is none to as whether it all comes from that date, or whether the first part is older. Many scholars hold the stories to be older, but do not agree amongst themselves as to the delimitation or the date of the earlier work. Meinhold held the earlier work to be the Aramaic part, while Dalman held it to consist of chaps. i–vi, a later redactor combining the two works by translating the first part of each from its original language into the other. Akin to this is Torrey's view that the author of vii–xii translated the beginning of the older work into Hebrew and wrote the first part of his own in Aramaic, in order to cement the two parts together. Hölscher argued that the earlier work consisted of chaps. i–vi, to which vii was added as an appendix. In the Maccabaean age this work was glossed, and the remaining chapters were added.

Very similarly Sellin regards i–vii as an older work, glossed and added to in the second century B.C. On the other hand, Haller holds chap. vii to be the oldest in the book. Chap. vii is held to be glossed or not according as it is attached to the pre-Maccabaean or to the Maccabaean part of the book, while chap. ii is also held by some to be glossed. In their assumed unglossed form both of these chapters are robbed of what is clearly their present point, and left with none that would offer a reasonable purpose for their composition. This uncertainty what to do with chapter vii exposes the weakness of the theories of division.

By its language the chapter is firmly linked to the first part of the book, while in its ideas and in the climax of its expectations it is linked both with chap. ii and with the later chapters. To every one of the stories of the first half point is given in the setting of the Maccabaean age, and the general aversion to the choice of a few Greek loan-words which contained within themselves pointed reference to the oppressor and his banquets, is most easily understood at this time. Hence the present writer adheres to the view that the book is a unity, and comes wholly from the Maccabaean age. It should be added that Torrey dates his earlier work *circa* 245 B.C., while chaps. i–vi are placed by Hölscher in the third century B.C., by Baumgartner in the Persian period, and by Welch in the Babylonian period, while Beek places chaps. i–vii in the Persian period.

(*b*) The origin of the bilingual character of the book is differently explained. Some views have been given in the preceding paragraph. To these others may be added. Bevan thought the whole was originally written in Hebrew, but a portion was lost and replaced by passages from an Aramaic translation, which had by now been made; Charles that the whole work was written in Aramaic, and the beginning and end were turned into Hebrew with a view to the inclusion of the work in the Canon. It is claimed by Charles that the hand of three translators can be detected, and he thinks they were hastily set to work within four years of the composition of the book.

The present writer believes that the stories were created one by one in Aramaic, and achieved an immediate popular success. Later the first of the visions was written similarly in Aramaic, but for the other visions, which are less suitable for popular circulation and intended for the student, Hebrew was used. Still later the stories and the visions were collected, and allowed to stand in a bilingual work, since all for whom the second part was written could read the first. But since the stories were now collected, the first was re-written to make it an introduction to them all—e.g., with Daniel's three friends introduced, in preparation for chap. iii—and re-written in the language of the later sections. The point of transition from the one language to the other was determined by the amount that needed to be re-written.

(*c*) The pseudonymity of the book is also differently counted for. It is held by many that the author resorted to it order to gain a hearing. This ignores the fact that the first h of the book is not pseudonymous. In it we have stories to about Daniel, with no suggestion that Daniel is himself tl author. Many writers have noted the indications that the stori of the first half were issued one by one, and therefore no questio of pseudonymity arises in connexion with them. If the autho had composed stories about Daniel which had achieved grea popularity, by writing his visions in the person of Daniel he could at once indicate the community of authorship of storie and visions, and could attach to the visions the prestige of the stories. In an age when title-pages were unknown his method was at once simple and effective.

(*d*) On the problem of the relation of the Daniel of this book to the Daniel of the book of Ezekiel (Ezek. xiv. 14, 20, xxviii. 3), some light has been shed by the Ras Shamra texts. It has long been argued that the Daniel of the book of Ezekiel could not have been a youthful contemporary of that prophet, since he is classed with Noah and Job, and that he must have been an ancient Oriental figure. Moreover, the name is spelt differently in Ezekiel and in this book. We have now a long text from Ras Shamra about Aqhat and his son Daniel, where the name is spelt as in Ezekiel, and it is probable that the Daniel of Ezekiel goes back to the figure of the Ras Shamra text, whose name had lingered on in tradition. It is not probable, however, that the Daniel of the book of Daniel has any connexion with this figure. For the stories that are told about him the author used older material, perhaps, and he had a kernel of inexact historical traditions of the sixth century B.C., but he adapted his material for a practical purpose and attached it to a figure of his own creation.

(c) each seems to exercise an authority independent of the other, that makes it most unlikely that they were contemporaries;

(d) whereas Nehemiah was contemporary with the high-priest Eliashib (Neh. iii. 1), Ezra was contemporary with Johanan (Ezra x. 6), Eliashib's grandson (Neh. xii. 11, 22);

(e) it is known from the Elephantine papyri (emanating from a Jewish colony in Egypt in the fifth century B.C., and found early in the present century) that Johanan was high-priest in 408 B.C.;

(f) it is known from the Elephantine papyri that the Jews in Egypt sought the help of Sanballat's sons in 408 B.C., and it is believed that this was because they administered affairs for their now aged father, who was, however, still governor, and that therefore Nehemiah, who was contemporary with Sanballat's active period, must be placed much earlier than this.

If the conclusion that Ezra belongs to the reign of Artaxerxes II is justified, he came to Jerusalem in 397 B.C. That we are carried down to a date even later than this for the work of the Chronicler, however, is probable. For the genealogy of 1 Chron. iii carries the Davidic line to the sixth generation after Zerubbabel, who lived *circa* 520 B.C. (extended to the eleventh generation in the Greek version). Moreover, the references to "the king of Persia" (Ezra i. 1, iii. 7, iv. 3, vii. 1) show that the Persian empire no longer exists, as is seen by comparison with the books of Haggai and Zechariah, and the Elephantine papyri, and also the sources employed in Ezra-Nehemiah, where we find "the king." We therefore arrive at a *terminus a quo* for the work of about 300 B.C., and many editors would place it somewhat later than this.

The work is written under the influence of P, and the history is sometimes rewritten to make it accord with the law of P, or judged from the standpoint of P. It ignores the northern kingdom, passes lightly over Saul, and aims above all things to make the story edifying. The older sources, as can be checked by a comparison of Samuel and Kings with Chronicles, are treated with great freedom where the compiler's interests are concerned. David's sin and misfortunes are ignored, and the troubles that accompanied the succession of Solomon are similarly passed over, and throughout there is a certain idealizing of history.

Nevertheless the Chronicler had access to sources not elsewhere preserved in the Old Testament, and where his particular interests are not concerned, it is probable that we may find some reliable supplementary material. On all that concerns the Temple liturgy in his own day, and especially on all that concerns the Temple music, he is a first-class authority, though in accordance with his general outlook he tends to throw back the conditions of his own day to an earlier day.

He refers to some of his sources, and others may be detected. These include the books of Samuel and Kings, and probably Isaiah, memoirs of Ezra and Nehemiah, Aramaic documents drawn on in the book of Ezra (of which iv. 8–vi. 18, and vii. 12–26 are in Aramaic), and probably Temple records and genealogical lists. There is much more disposition to-day to treat with respect the Aramaic documents than was formerly the case, and it is possible that they were taken over together with the connecting Aramaic verses from an earlier Aramaic work dealing with the period, though Kapelrud rejects the authenticity of Ezra vii. 12–26, and attributes the whole of the Ezra memoirs directly to the Chronicler, denying that he rested on any genuine source. If he drew on an older Aramaic work, it could not be placed earlier than the fourth century, as can be established on linguistic grounds. The Chronicler further names "The Midrash of the Book of Kings" (2 Chron. xxiv. 27), and "The Midrash of Iddo the Seer" (2 Chron. xiii. 22), amongst his sources, though some scholars would identify these.

Recent work has shown that if this statement of the final editing of Chronicles-Ezra-Nehemiah is correct, it is incomplete. For a stage intermediate between the sources of the work and its present state must be postulated. Von Rad has demonstrated the work of two hands in the book, the one writing under the influence of D and the other under the influence of P, and this has been taken up by Welch in two important publications. Welch denied the unity of authorship of Chronicles-Ezra-Nehemiah, finding a double recension in Chronicles, and assigning the first to a date *circa* 520 B.C., and the second to a writer influenced by P. He further accused the author of Ezra-Nehemiah of perverting valuable sources by his misleading arrangement of them. Neh. x he assigns to the improbably early date 586 B.C., and Ezra he unduly depreciates. In the early years of the present century Torrey argued with great vigour for the view that Ezra is a purely fictitious character, but this view has secured little following. Finally, the view of Rothstein and Hänel may be mentioned, according to which the groundwork of the Chronicler was written *circa* 432 B.C., and revised *circa* 400 B.C., and subsequently interpolated. For the date of the first draft of the book, this view is more probable than Welch's, but the present writer would place the revision based on P nearer to 300 B.C.

BOOK V

THE CANON

CHAPTER XXII

THE GROWTH AND FIXATION OF THE CANON

IT has been commonly supposed that the Canon of the Old Testament came into being in three stages, corresponding to the three divisions of the Hebrew Bible, so that first the Law was received as Scripture and its limits fixed, and then the Prophets, while the miscellaneous collection of the writings continued to be open to fresh additions until a yet later time. This view is still presented by Pfeiffer, who puts the canonization of the Law at *circa* 400 B.C., of the Prophets at *circa* 200 B.C., and the final definition of the writings at *circa* A.D. 90 (the Council of Jamnia). In favour of this view it is urged that the prophetic Canon must have been closed before the book of Daniel was written, or it would have been included in that division.

Oesterley and Robinson, however, following Hölscher, maintain that there was no Canon of the Old Testament until the Council of Jamnia, when the leaders of the Jews gathered there are known to have discussed which books "defiled the hands" by reason of their sacredness. Before this time there had been veneration for certain books, but it is improper to speak of them as a Canon.

Both of these views seem unduly simple. The Samaritans recognize the Pentateuch, and only the Pentateuch, as Scripture. That its limits must have been so firmly fixed before the final breach between Jews and Samaritans that no further additions could take place is therefore certain. This then already was a Canon, and there is every reason to allow that the Law first became canonical. We know of no formal decision arrived at in council, but that is not the fundamental process of canonization. As soon as books have attained such a position in the veneration of men that they are regarded as authoritative, and their text not to be changed, they are properly to be spoken of as a Canon.

Pfeiffer's date for this is perhaps unduly early, but it should certainly be placed somewhere in the fourth century B.C.

So far as the rest of the Old Testament is concerned, it is to be observed that the New Testament offers evidence that most of it could be appealed to as authoritative before the Council of Jamnia met, and it appears to have been known by its threefold division (Luke xxiv. 44). Yet in the first century A.D. it is known that the limits of neither the Latter Prophets nor the writings were held to be irrevocably fixed, since there was discussion as to whether Ezekiel and the Song of Songs should be accepted as canonical. In both cases the discussed book had already secured such a hold in men's esteem that it could not be dislodged, and the result of the discussion was not to make it canonical, but to confirm its canonicity.

It is, indeed, doubtful how far it is correct to speak of the Council of Jamnia. We know of discussions that took place there amongst the Rabbis, but we know of no formal or binding decisions that were made, and it is probable that the discussions were informal, though none the less helping to crystallize and to fix more firmly the Jewish tradition.

Speaking generally, the divisions of the Hebrew Canon correspond to different types of writings, and few books in the miscellaneous collection of the Writings would be expected to be placed in the earlier divisions, quite apart from any question of date. It might, however, have been expected that Ruth would stand with the Former Prophets, and similarly Chronicles-Ezra-Nehemiah. It might also have been expected that Daniel would stand with the Latter Prophets. It is probable that the Former Prophets had already achieved so firm a place, by the subtle process of growing veneration, that they are properly spoken of as a Canon before the book of Ruth had achieved anything like such an esteem. It need not be supposed that Ruth was not written until the Canon of the Former Prophets was fixed, but that the time when it was being treasured as sacred was later than that at which they had received general recognition. So far as Chronicles-Ezra-Nehemiah is concerned, the same thing is probably true, that they came too late to find a place in a collection that had become, by general consent and not by formal decision, firmly defined.

So far as the book of Daniel is concerned, it is possible that at the time when it was written the collection of the Latter Prophets had attained relative fixity, and the evidence of Ben Sira (Ecclus. xlviii f.) would suggest that this was so. It might have been supposed in that case, however, that some two centuries and more later there would have been no doubt whatever about the book of Ezekiel. It is therefore possible that Daniel was placed among the Writings because it was felt to be *sui generis*, and not like any of the other prophetic books. The stories of its first half might seem to have something in common with the book of Jonah, and the visions of its second half something in common with those of the book of Zechariah. Yet here we find no prophetic oracles introduced with a "Thus saith the Lord," and no statement that "the word of the Lord came to Daniel," such as we find in even Jonah and Zechariah. It may also have been known in the second century B.C., when the book of Daniel achieved its fame, that although the book presented a message from God, its hero was a fictitious character, whereas the prophets were all believed to be historical characters —as Daniel was in due course believed to be.

It may therefore be assumed, though it cannot be finally proved, that the crystallization of sacred books into the divisions of the Hebrew Canon was imperceptibly going on during the last pre-Christian centuries, and that the processes for the different divisions overlapped, but reached relative completion for the Law first, for the former Prophets next, for the Latter Prophets next, and finally for the Writings. That even the Writings had become more or less fixed by the first century B.C. is suggested by the failure of the Psalms of Solomon to secure entry. The achievement of relative fixity might prevent new works securing recognition, without fixing the text, and the evidence of the Greek version of such a book as Jeremiah is of importance here. That the canonization of the Law was absolute, if informal, before the end of the fourth century B.C. may be taken as certain; that the canonization of both prophetic collections was generally accepted, even if less absolutely, by about 200 B.C. is very probable; and that the admission of any fresh book to the Canon of the Writings after 100 B.C. would have had to face formidable obstacles is also probable, though there may have been a greater measure of fluidity within the group of works which had secured some measure of recognition by then, so that not all circles recognized all the books that others recognized.

That yet other books were acquiring a measure of sanctity in some Jewish circles is proved by the presence of some further works in Greek manuscripts of the Old Testament. These are printed in the Apocrypha in our Bibles. The manuscripts that contain them are Christian manuscripts, of which the earliest are much later than the Council of Jamnia. Yet the books are Jewish books, and they were taken over by the Church from the Jews. There is no evidence that they were ever recognized as canonical Jewish Scriptures, or that their claims to canonicity were so much as discussed at Jamnia, and in the Christian Church they were by no means universally recognized as canonical. A whole series of early Fathers denied that they should be treated as part of the Canon, while recognizing their value for edification. Yet gradually they established themselves in the Church alongside the other books, and in the Greek manuscripts, where the divisions of the Hebrew Canon were ignored and books redistributed, these were distributed through the collection.

It is therefore probable that the collection of these books was begun by Jews, and that they were acquiring a measure of sanctity, but that this process was stopped by the discussions of the Jewish Canon at Jamnia. The Christians were not bound by the Council of Jamnia, however, and if they had already taken over the sacred books of the Jews, with this looser collection on the fringe, the process of growth in veneration could continue amongst them, as it did, until they were securely established. Jerome and others held that only the Hebrew Canon should be regarded as the true Canon, and even after these books had secured general recognition and been approved by Councils, voices continued to be raised against their recognition. The general rejection of them by the Protestant Churches may have contributed to their firmer recognition by the Roman Church at the Council of Trent. Even since that Council there have been Catholic doubts expressed about them, while with the Protestant Churches rejection has never been universal and absolute.

In modern times there has been a growing interest, not alone in these books, but in certain others, commonly, though not very satisfactorily, referred to as Pseudepigrapha. Catholic writers, who accept the canonicity of the former class, and who do not therefore refer to them as Apocrypha (=Hidden books), often refer to these Pseudepigrapha as Apocrypha. The terminology is therefore somewhat confusing, and Torrey has recently advocated the use of the term Apocrypha to cover all the books which stand outside the Hebrew Canon of the Old Testament, and which are included under either of the terms Apocrypha or Pseudepigrapha. This whole literature is of great interest as showing the trends and varieties of Jewish literary work during the closing centuries of the pre-Christian era and the first century of the Christian era, though it would still need to be supplemented by the works of Philo and Josephus. The writings of the Apocrypha and Pseudepigrapha have closer affinities with the writings of the Old Testament, however. They include some excellent historical writing, such as 1 and 2 Maccabees (two independent works, and not parts of a single work, like the books of Samuel), and important literature of the Wisdom class, such as Ecclesiasticus and Wisdom, and other works of great value to the student, and especially those with an apocalyptic interest, such as Enoch, Jubilees, the Testaments of the Twelve Patriarchs, and 4 Ezra (2 Esdras).

It is in the light of these fringes, both those which secured recognition in the Christian Church but not in the Synagogue that gave them birth, and those which failed to secure a place in the Christian Church, that we can see the process of canonization illustrated, and realize how complex and subtle it was. And we are warned against any simple and schematic theory of the establishment of the Canon of the Old Testament. Like the growth of a tree, which passes imperceptibly from the stage of a sapling that might be transplanted to the stage when it is impossible to remove it, save by felling, canonicity grew imperceptibly. For a new work to secure a place in a given collection became progressively more difficult, though we cannot define with precision the point when it became impossible. And the different collections, which began their life at different times, reached and passed that indefinable point at different times.

By comparison with these other writings the true greatness of the Old Testament is seen the more clearly. Its own level is uneven, as also is the level of these other works, and there are passages in the Apocrypha and Pseudepigrapha which could be exchanged without loss for passages in the Old Testament. Yet as a whole they cannot be compared with the Old Testament, and the Christian Church can share with Judaism in the recognition of her debt to the experience and the spiritual penetration of those who bequeathed this precious heritage to the world, and yet more to the God Who mediated through them the secrets of His heart.

SHORT LIST OF BOOKS FOR FURTHER READING

A. GENERAL

C. Cornill, *Introduction to the Canonical Books of the Old Testament*, 1907 (London: Williams and Norgate).
A good statement of the more radical positions of its time.

S. R. Driver, *An Introduction to the Literature of the Old Testament*, 9th ed., 1913 (Edinburgh: T. & T. Clark).
Despite its age this is in some respects still not superseded, because of the fullness of its treatment, and the sobriety of its judgment.

G. B. Gray, *A Critical Introduction to the Old Testament*, 1913 (London: Duckworth).
Much briefer than Driver, and less conservative. Like all books of its age, it needs much supplementing.

J. A. Bewer, *The Literature of the Old Testament in its Historical Development*, 1922, 2nd ed., 1933 (New York: Columbia University Press).
Treats of the books in the order of their writing, instead of following the order of either the Hebrew or the English Bible.

E. Sellin, *Introduction to the Old Testament*, 1923 (London: Hodder & Stoughton).
The work of a very stimulating scholar, more conservative than Cornill. But Sellin's positions on many books were modified in later German editions.

C. F. Kent, *The Growth and Contents of the Old Testament*, 1926 (London: John Murray).
Consists in the main of the introductory chapters of the author's volumes of "The Student's Old Testament."

J. E. McFadyen, *Introduction to the Old Testament*, New ed., 1932 (London: Hodder & Stoughton).
Brief and well written.

W. O. E. Oesterley and T. H. Robinson, *An Introduction to the Books of the Old Testament*, 1934 (London: S.P.C.K.).
A standard book, on a smaller scale than Driver, but more up-to-date. Especially good on the prophetic books.

H. W. Robinson, *The Old Testament : its Making and Meaning*, 1937 (London: University of London Press).
Very brief, but marked by the sobriety of judgment and penetration that distinguished all the author's work.

R. H. Pfeiffer, *Introduction to the Old Testament*, 1941 (New York: Harpers), 2nd edition, 1952 (London: Black).
On a larger scale than any of the foregoing, and well abreast of modern work. Indispensable for advanced study. More radical in some ways than many recent works. An abridged edition appeared in 1957.

Stanley Cook, *An Introduction to the Bible*, 1945 (London: Penguin Books).
Covering a much wider field than the present work, this little book is packed with information, and is strongly to be commended.

G. F. Moore, *The Literature of the Old Testament*, revised by L. H. Brockington, 1948 (Oxford: Geoffrey Cumberlege).
A long valued and still valuable work, somewhat slightly revised, without taking much account of the work of the past generation.

A. Bentzen, *Introduction to the Old Testament*, Vol. I, *The Canon of the Old Testament, The Text of the Old Testament, The Forms of Old Testament Literature*, 1948; Vol. II, *The Books of the Old Testament*, 1949 (Copenhagen: G. E. C. Gad).
A most valuable treatment of the subjects with which it deals, and especially for its treatment of the forms of the literature. The second volume contains the special introduction to the individual books. Particularly useful for its use of Scandinavian literature not easily accessible.

B. SPECIAL

1. *Recent Criticism*

J. E. McFadyen, "The Present Position of Old Testament Criticism," in *The People and the Book* (ed. A. S. Peake), 1925 (Oxford: Clarendon Press).
A good survey of work to that date.

J. Hempel, "The Forms of Oral Tradition" and "The Contents of the Literature" in *Record and Revelation* (ed. H. W. Robinson), 1938 (Oxford: Clarendon Press), and

O. Eissfeldt, "Modern Criticism," in *Record and Revelation*.
These are masterly essays, by two of the most eminent of living German scholars.

G. A. Barton, "The Present State of Old Testament Studies," in *The Haverford Symposium on Archaeology and the Bible*, 1938 (New Haven: American Schools of Oriental Research).
Useful to supplement the preceding essays.

J. Coppens, *The Old Testament and the Critics*, 1942 (Paterson, N. J. St. Anthony Guild).
A critical survey of the history of criticism, particularly Pentateuchal Criticism, by a distinguished Catholic scholar. His positions are more conservative than those of the present book, but his survey is of the greatest value. A more recent edition in French has expanded the non-Pentateuchal portion.

H. F. Hahn, *The Old Testament in Modern Research*, 1956, (London, S.C.M.)
A valuable supplement to the following work. It covers a longer period and is in some respects wider in scope, though in others narrower.

H H. Rowley (ed. by), *The Old Testament and Modern Study*, 1951 (Oxford: Clarendon Press).
This volume, published since the present work appeared, contains in chapters ii-vii an invaluable account of modern work on Old Testament Introduction, and should be used to supplement the foregoing works.

2. *The Pentateuch and Historical Books*

J. E. Carpenter and G. Harford, *The Composition of the Hexateuch*, 1902 (London: Longmans, Green).

The fullest exposition in English of the Graf-Wellhausen view and still of the greatest value for the study of that view, though it should be followed by the study of Coppens' book for more recent challenges.

A. T. Chapman, *An Introduction to the Pentateuch*, 1911 (Cambridge: University Press).

Careful and reliable; smaller than the preceding, and like it, too early to deal with modern challenges.

D. C. Simpson, *Pentateuchal Criticism*, 1914, 2nd ed., 1924 (London: Hodder & Stoughton).

The best introduction to the critical view for the non-technical reader. The second edition is but a reprint of the first, and is, in any case, too early to take account of all the recent activity in this field.

C. A. Simpson, *The Early Traditions of Israel*, 1948 (Oxford, Basil Blackwell).

A most elaborate examination of the J1, the J2 and the E documents, as they are delimited by the author. The remaining documents of the Pentateuch are not treated in detail. Unfortunately much subjective matter is included, and the arrangement makes it hard to see the wood for the trees.

C. A. Simpson, *Composition of the Book of Judges*, 1958 (Oxford, Blackwell).

Similar to the preceding work, and carrying the analysis further. The same major sources are found here.

3. *The Prophets*

T. H. Robinson, *Prophecy and the Prophets in Ancient Israel*, 1924 (London: Duckworth).

An excellent interpretation of the prophets, by one who has contributed more than any living British writer to their study:

J. M. P. Smith, *The Prophets and their Times*, 1925 (Chicago: University Press).

Also very good. Neither the preceding work nor this can bring the reader up-to-date, however.

J. M. P. Smith, *The Prophets and their Times*, 2nd ed., revised by W. A. Irwin, 1941 (Chicago: University Press).
Many of the chapters have been completely rewritten, so that this is really a new work.

R. B. Y. Scott, *The Relevance of the Prophets*, 1944 (New York: Macmillan).
Does not deal with the making of the prophetic books, but is a first-class treatment of the message and significance of the prophets.

4. *The Psalms*

G. B. Gray, *The Forms of Hebrew Poetry*, 1915 (London: Hodder & Stoughton).
The best treatment in English of Hebrew poetic forms, both reviewing the work of others and making an independent contribution to the subject.

A. R. Johnson, *Sacral Kingship in Ancient Israel*, 1955 (Cardiff, University of Wales Press).
An important study of the place of the King in the ritual of the Jerusalem cultus.

D. C. Simpson (ed. by), *The Psalmists*, 1926 (Oxford: University Press).
A series of lectures by distinguished authorities, of the greatest value.

W. O. E. Oesterley, *A Fresh Approach to the Psalms*, 1937 (London Ivor Nicholson & Watson).
Good assembly of material on the Psalms, embodying much from modern work, though not offering any systematic exposition of the leading modern contributors.

F. James, *Thirty Psalmists*, 1938 (New York: Putnam).
Chiefly interesting as an exposition of Gunkel's method.

T. H. Robinson, *The Poetry of the Old Testament*, 1947 (London: Duckworth).
An excellent introduction to the poetical books of the Old Testament, issued as a companion to Professor Robinson's work on the prophets. It therefore deals with much more than the Psalms. There is a first-class bibliography prepared by Professor A. R. Johnson.

5. *The Wisdom Literature*

H. Ranston, *The Old Testament Wisdom Books and their Teaching*, 1930 (London: Epworth Press).
   Of the highest value, and strongly to be recommended.

O. S. Rankin, *Israel's Wisdom Literature*, 1936 (Edinburgh: T. & T. Clark).
   An excellent exposition of the thought of the Wisdom writers.

NOTE.   Only works written in English are included in this Bibliography.   Students who wish to keep abreast of foreign as well as English work should consult the annual Book List of the Society for Old Testament Study, obtainable from the Publications Secretary, Rev. George Farr, 10 Chandos Road, Chorlton-cum-Hardy, Manchester, 21.

INDEX

(a) Subject

181

Moabite stone, 74
Monarchy, Establishment of, 64 f.
Mosaic authorship of Pentateuch rejected, 16 ff.
Moses, 15 f., 17, 22 f., 26 f., 39, 41, 42 f., 49, 53, 59, 97, 124, 135; Blessing of, 40 f.; Song of, 42, 127

NABOPOLASSAR, 120
Nabonidus, 156 f.
Nahum, 116 f., 120
Naphtali, Tribe of, 60 f.
Nathan, 84, 114
Nebuchadrezzar, 73, 102, 156 f.
Nehemiah, 35, 99, 102, 123 f., 132, 151, 162 ff.; book of, 11, 49, 51, 162 ff., 170
New Covenant, 102
New Year Festival, 132
Nicanor, 154 f.
Nineveh, 114, 116 f., 120
Noah, 18, 21, 38, 161
Numbers, Book of, 16

OBADIAH, 112 f.
Omri, 74
Ostraca, 85, 102 f., 108
Othniel, 58

PADDAN-ARAM, 17, 19
Passover, 30
Peniel, 17
Pentateuch, 11, 15 ff., 169; Mosaic authorship rejected 16 ff.; sources of, 23, 25; J 25 f., 28, 31 f., 34, 36, 37 ff., 41, 42 ff., 50, 54 ff., 58, 60, 66; J₁ 42 f.; J₂, 42 f.; L, 43, 54, 60, 66; S, 43; K, 43; E, 25 f., 28, 31 ff., 34, 36, 37 ff., 41, 45, 50, 54 ff., 60, 66; D, 25 ff., 28, 31 ff., 42, 44, 54 f., 123, 164; H, 27 f., 35 f.; P, 25 f., 27, 28, 29, 33 ff., 39, 43 ff., 50, 54 f., 66, 123, 163 ff.
Persians, 40, 72, 121 f., 152
Pharaoh, 17
Philistines, 17, 64 f.
Pirqe Aboth, 137
Poetry, Character of Hebrew, 127 ff.; Parallelism, 127 f.; Rhythm, 128, 151; Stanzas, 129

Potiphar, 19
Pragmatism, 27, 58, 72
Priests, 26 f., 28, 31, 33, 39, 123
Prophecy, Nature of, 79 ff.
Prophets, Cultic, 80 f., 111, 118; of Baal, 80; compilation of books of, 84 ff.
Proverbs, 11, 137 ff., 140 ff.
Psalms, 11, 118, 130 ff.; cultic use of, 134; Headings of, 135 f.; Types of, 134 f.; Babylonian, 132
Psalms of Solomon, 131, 133, 171
Pseudepigrapha, 173
Purim, 154 f.

RAS SHAMRA, 34, 127, 132 f., 161
Rebekah, 19, 38, 41
Remnant, 94, 112
Reuben, 26; tribe of, 39
Ruth, 11, 150 f.; 170

SAMARITAN SCHISM, 35, 148, 169
Samuel, 45, 58 f., 64 ff.; books of, 11, 49, 51, 60, 65 ff., 71, 75 f., 93, 163 f., 173
Samson, 58
Sanballat, 163
Sarai, 21
Satan, 143
Saul, 17, 32, 40 f., 53, 58 f., 62, 64 ff., 68, 70, 163
Scythian question, 119 n.
Selah, 118
Sennacherib, 74, 90
Servant Songs, 96 ff.
Seth, 21
Shaddai, see Divine names
Shamgar, 58
Shechem, 26
Shem, 38
Shiloh, 62, 64
Shulammite, 148 f.
Sihon, 38
Simeon, Tribe of, 39, 41
Sinai, 49
Sisera, 56, 60 f.
Smerdis, pseudo, 121
Sodom, 88
Solomon, 29, 45, 55 f., 71, 75, 140, 148 f., 152, 154, 163
Solomon, Acts of, 73

(b) Authors

(c) Scripture

THE GROWTH OF THE OLD TESTAMENT

by H. H. ROWLEY

"The author has efficiently accomplished his purpose of presenting a fair picture of the state of present-day opinion on the growth of the Old Testament. . . . It presents clearly in brief compass the viewpoints of contemporary scholarship without being merely a compendium of opinions. It is concise, accurate, and readable, and it will be useful as a quick reference for those who want to be brought up to date in biblical scholarship."—*The Journal of Biblical Literature*

"Without omitting anything of real importance to the student, he has achieved a marvel of skilful compression, giving in less than 200 pages a clearly arranged, lucidly expounded, account of how this amazing collection of a nation's literature came into being and received the shape in which we have it today. Recent development̲s ̲ ̲-̲ary and historical criticism are put befor̲ ̲ ̲ ̲ ̲ ̲ ̲h̲ a just appraisement of their ̲ ̲ ̲ ̲ ̲ ̲ ̲ ̲e̲. The book should be widely ̲ ̲ ̲ ̲ ̲ ̲ ̲ ̲ ̲ ̲Old Testament is a subject of study."—̲ ̲ ̲ ̲ ̲r̲d̲i̲a̲n̲ (Manchester)

Contents

I. The Law: The Pentateuch.

II. The Former Prophets: The Hebrew Historian and his Purpose; The Book of Joshua; The Book of Judges; The Books of Samuel; The Books of Kings.

III. The Latter Prophets: The Nature of Prophecy; Compilation of the Prophetic Books; The Book of Isaiah; The Book of Jeremiah; The Book of Ezekiel; The Book of the Twelve.

IV. The Writings: The Character of Hebrew Poetry; The Psalms; The Hebrew Wisdom Literature; The Book of Proverbs; The Book of Job; The Five Rolls; The Book of Daniel; Chronicles—Ezra—Nehemiah.

V. The Canon: Growth and Fixation.

HARPER & ROW, PUBLISHERS

COVER DESIGN BY URI SHULEVITZ